INCITING REFLECTION
MUSINGS ON
MATTERS OF LIFE

ROB
SIMON

INCITING REFLECTION
Robert Simon

COMMON GROUND PUBLISHING
Since 2017
1736 Womer Drive
Wichita, Kansas 67203

Publishing History:
New Edition published 2020 by Common Ground Publishing Hard cover edition published July 2018 by B.Global Publishing under the auspices of Positive Rhythm Productions.

Market test version published 2002 by Common Man Publishing under the auspices of Positive Rhythm Productions.

Copyright © 2002, 2018, 2020 by Robert Simon
Positive Rhythm Productions
1736 Womer Drive - Wichita, Kansas 67203

Bulk quantities of this book are available at special discount purchase prices to be used for promotions, special premiums, fund-raising and educational needs. For details, contact the publisher or the author.

Front Cover Design by Dustin Parker & Rob Simon
Interior design by FormattedBooks

All rights reserved. This book, or parts thereof, may not be reproduced in any form without permission.

An application to register this book for cataloging has been submitted to the Library of Congress.

ISBN: 978-1-954302-00-6 (Hardback)
ISBN: 978-1-954302-01-3 (Paperback)
ISBN: 978-1-954302-02-0 (E-book)

Printed in the United States of America
3 4 5 6 7 8 9 10

CONTENTS

Preface vii

"SEEING" 1

I See..3
Perspectives, Perceptions and Peacemaking 5
"Simplexity"..9
No Difference in The Dark...13
Highest Common Denominator 15
The Human Continent..19
Neither Islands Nor City-States Be 23
Theories of Relativity..25
The Proof Is In The Proof? 27
A Paradigm for Life 29
The Paradigm of Jigsaw Puzzles 33

PEOPLE IN OUR PERISCOPES 37

My Brothers 39
People Are Like Clouds 41
It Is Not "It"...45
Whose Show Is This Anyway?..47
From The Director's Chair...51
The Brilliant Server 53
More On The Brilliant Server 57
Inhumanity..61
A Case For The Golden Rule 63

NEW YEARS, NEW LIVES, NEW VIEWS, AND OTHER CELEBRATIONS............65

Stranger's Eyes............67
Reflections on "THE" Holidays 69
Thanksgiving 365............71
Giving Thanks for EVERYthing 75
H.A.P.P.Y. N.E.W. Y.E.A.R. 77
Self-Affirmations............81
Reaffirming Relationships 85
Distant Replay............87
On Black History Month............91
A New Story of Christmas............93
A Twist on
Christmas Themes 97

EXERCISING OUR LOVE MUSCLES............99

Love Comes First............101
Give Yourself A Valentine 103
Intimate Friends............107
A Heart So Big............111
Multilingual Love............115
Unconditional Love............119
The Necessity of Unconditional Love............123
The Three L's............127

DECIPHERING LIFE'S PUZZLES 131

C H A N N E L............133
When We Assume About Each Other 135
Serendipity?............137
Life Imitates Art!............139
The Band-Aid Adventure............141
When Your "Get Up And Go" Gets Up And Goes............143
The New A.M.N.E.S.I.A.............145
How To Love a Hater 147
Above The Clouds 149

Chasing Hunches 151

ON GOD AND GODLINGS 153

Wee Hour Meditation 155
Cosmic Toys: Battery Powered 157
A Matter of Spirit 161
The Content of Spirit 165
Praying Together 169
Faith 171
Agitations: Of Water And Spirit 173
Doubt or Faith 177
Subtle Energies 181

PRESSING ON WHEN THE PRESSURE'S ON 183

Silent Alarm 185
Stress Versus Reinhold Niebuhr 187
Why Worry? 191
Psychic Safety 193
Late-in', Waitin', Hurryin', and Worryin' 197
When The Weight Gets Lifted 201
Burning Both Ends of the Candle 205
Carry On 209

SUCCESS: SELF-SEARCHING, AND SINGLEMINDEDNESS 211

Who Are We? 213
Why We Can All Be Successful 215
Watermelon Seeds 217
The Inn Is Not Home 219
Being On Fire 223
Blood, Sweat and Tears 225
Do It Today 227
Priorities Again 229
Needing Help 231

BUILDING PEOPLE; BUILDING COMMUNITIES.............................233

Slice of Life 235
Refounding The Village...237
Privilege and Responsibility 241
From Pennies To Millions 243
Welfare or "Well Fair?"..245
An APB For Rites of Passage..247
Youth Employment 249
Do What You Can,..251
Play..255

CAVEATS AND FOOTNOTES 259

Boomerang 261
Either/Or; or And/And? 263
Fight, Flight or Flow..265
Conditional Expectations 267
Hidden Agendas..269
The Trap of Routines 271
The Obsession With Convenience 273
What I Learned When I Was Eleven 277

BONUS SECTION.. 279

Tossed Salad: A View of a Multicultural America 281

PREFACE

It is said by some that perhaps we think too much. We are often so busy forcing thoughts through our minds that we rarely take time for listening to our inner voice—which some say is the real source of wisdom.

We apply great exuberance to thoughts geared to the management of everyday crises—big and small. Because of that, we seldom make the time to use our minds for things that may matter even more.

We spend a great deal of energy wrestling mentally with the various circumstances of our lives. As a result, we miss opportunities to calmly apply a meditative state to life's onslaughts in the same way a martial artist might maneuver to deflect a flurry of attempted blows.

If we could be mentally quiet enough, our concerns might simply undo themselves when the force of their intention meets the counter-balance of our calm.

There are others who say maybe we don't think enough. The casual observer of everyday life can easily discover instances where choices are seemingly made with no regard for thought whatsoever. Responses to events in our experience are often no better than the kind of knee-jerk reactions that are the result of the classic reflex test done with a tiny hammer just beneath the knee cap. We sometimes let our emotions, or our prejudices, or our apathy, or our indifference rule our choices rather than to expend the energy required to think our way to what may be a far better selection.

Still, there are some who say that it is not so much the <u>quantity</u> of our thinking that is the issue. Instead, when we <u>do</u> choose to think, our thoughts leave much to be desired in terms of <u>quality</u>. We do not think critically, they say. We do not think logically. We do not think intuitively. We do not think holistically. We do not think carefully. We do not think well.

I'm inclined to believe that all of these views may be correct—at least at times. Sometimes we think too much. Sometimes we don't think enough. And sometimes, when we think, we might just as well not because our thinking is a tricycle where a high-powered sports car is required.

Part of the problem, is that most of us are never <u>taught</u> to think. What's worse is that some of us are not <u>allowed</u> to think. Parents, teachers, ministers, government leaders and many other leaders are famous for choosing to think <u>for</u> us rather than encouraging and allowing us to think for <u>ourselves</u>. Then to make matters even worse, as others are willing to do our thinking for us, most of us are content to let it happen—unless we somehow receive a negative benefit from the allowance. When <u>that</u> occurs, we get <u>really</u> interested in independent thought; but we have been too <u>dependent</u> and find ourselves well short of the amount of practice we need for going our own intellectual way.

Sometimes I think it would be helpful to attach a special banner or sticker to every street sign in the world's towns that simply says, "**Thinking Allowed.**" Maybe if we are reminded of it often enough it will start to sink subliminally into our subconscious and we'll thirst for opportunities to think as much as we thirst for water. But I won't hold my breath waiting for that fantasy to come true.

I'm taking matters into my own hands, instead. I'm choosing this modest beginning on a campaign to incite reflection. Will you join me in a commitment to that? If enough of us decide to become rabble-rousers for earnest thought and meditation, we have a chance. If enough of us become teachers and encouragers of a process that allows us to carefully, positively and productively fix our minds and hearts on the subjects and concerns of our lives, we may yet find enough wisdom to survive. Personally, I don't even mind inciting a riot—if it is a riot of meaningful thought!

Come on! Let's stir up some brain waves! But let's be sure that they are contemplative waves. Let's be certain they are deliberate waves. Let's insist that they be creative waves. Let's push for positive, powerful and respectful waves. And let's be advocates for <u>intermittent</u> waves which allow some quiet between our bursts of powerful thought. It is in the silences when thoughts are not pressing on the edges of our brains that the fruits of our thinking can best be realized.

Robert Simon, 2017

I SEE

I see...
Not just with eyes,
But with ears and hands
And nostrils
And taste buds
And the hairs
On the back of my neck.

I see...
With heart...so intensely
And mind...so immensely
And more than I want to at times.

I see...
In the mirrors
Of my mind
Reflections of
My experience
Through the mists
Of my memory.

I see...
Through the eyes
Of those who see me
Differently
Than I do myself.

I see...
With the heart
Of one who loves...
Sometimes
Too much,
And who lives
Sometimes
Too much
In the moment --
Or not enough in it.

I see...
On the dreamscape
Of my thoughts
A vision
Of a life
Where I get more
Only to give more.

I see...
Therefore I know
What there is to see
And still
Know not what
I see.

PERSPECTIVES, PERCEPTIONS AND PEACEMAKING
(LESSONS FROM AN ELEPHANT)

There is a beautiful allegory from an Eastern tradition which provides a wonderful demonstration of the difficulties that arise when people have differing views of a perceived reality. I have remembered it as a fable called "The Five Blind Men and The Elephant." There is, however, a wonderful poem by John G. Saxe called "The Blind Men and the Elephant" which features <u>six</u> "men of Indostan."

My version of the story, in a nutshell, is that five blind men encounter an elephant for the first time and begin to explore it through their sense of touch. One approaches the elephant from behind and is brushed by the elephant's tail. He grabs it; and, upon discovering that it is long and slender and bushy on the lower end, promptly announces to his comrades that the elephant is very much like a broom…because, after all, he is familiar with brooms.

Meanwhile, another of the men walked up to one of the elephant's sides and, reaching out, felt the broad expanse of its hide in every direction he reached—up, down and to his left and right. <u>He</u> then reported that the elephant was very much like a wall because, of course, he <u>knew</u> about walls.

Only a few feet away, however, another blind man had decided, first, to get down on one knee; and when he did this, he discovered one of the elephant's legs. Eventually, he discovered that it was roughly cylindrical, big enough that he could barely reach around it with both arms, and that it extended to the ground and stopped. He announced to his companions that the elephant was very much like a tree. After all, trees were things with which he was quite familiar.

And yet, almost within his arm's reach was the fourth blind man who detected one of the elephant's tusks. In his estimation, the long, hard, smooth, curved shape which ended in a rather sharp point was reminiscent of a saber. So perhaps for lack of a better model with which he could compare the elephant he was learning about, he declared that the animal was very much like a saber. No doubt, he and his friends were all familiar with this very common device of battle.

Finally, the fifth sightless man had begun his exploration of the elephant by being all but attacked by the pachyderm himself. The elephant had reached out to him with his trunk. The man subsequently discovered the creature as one which was long, and slender, and moist, and rough to the touch, and given to a familiar wiggling motion almost all the time. It was an easy diagnosis for him that this elephant was, indeed, very much like a snake. Because of his previous experience, of that fact, he could be sure.

The allegory ends at this point with this rhetorical question: Who was right; and who was wrong? The apparent answer is that they were all right and they were all wrong.

At this first moment of encounter, they each had a view of the beast that was narrow and incomplete. Obviously, if the learning for each of them ends at the same place it began, none of them will truly know what an elephant is and will probably consider the views of each of the others to be totally, and irrevocably in error.

A great misfortune in our world today is that many of us are very much like the blind men in this story. We have perceptions, in which we are totally invested, to which we are totally committed, but for which we are depending on a unique perspective. These tailor-made viewpoints may not be shared by those who are not able to see life's circumstances through our eyes and from inside our shoes. One of society's most enduring core questions has to do with whether or not we can get most people to continue to "walk around the elephant."

Our Native American brothers understood this need as well as anyone when, like Edwin Laughing Fox, some had been thoughtful enough to pray. **"O, Great Spirit, help me not to judge another until I have walked two**

weeks in their moccasins." Or as the singer, Joe South, sang more recently: **"Hey, before you abuse, criticize and accuse, walk a mile in my shoes!"**

If we are to ever establish tolerance, understanding, a collaborative spirit, and peace on this earth we must somehow internalize the spirit of the prayer and the common sense of the lyric.

"SIMPLEXITY"
(HOW TO GET A GRIP ON THINGS)

The next time you're faced with a problem that seems unbelievably complex, and difficult to handle, ask yourself the question: "How can I see this difficulty more simply?" You may find that asking <u>this</u> question begins to provide an answer to the troublesome one.

Practically anything that you can view can be viewed at a level of complexity or at a level of simplicity.

Take a moment to look at something right in front of you. It could be your coffee mug, this book, your computer screen, your hand, the top of your desk, a sink full of dishes, the steering wheel of your car—whatever. The item you choose has a basic meaning for you. You have a name for it, a purpose perhaps, and maybe a feeling about it such as indifferent, pleased, thankful, joyful, frustrated, angry, disgusted, or upset.

But beyond that simple recognizance and that basic meaning is a complexity that almost defies comprehension. Think for a moment about the history of the item you've chosen. From where did the raw materials for it come? How were they gathered and/or transported to a location where they could be formed into the object or objects you see? What had to be bought or sold in order for it to exist? Who designed it? Who designed the first of its kind? How did that person come up with the idea?

What is its purpose? Who decided that it would function in that capacity? Who decided that such a function was important? Why wasn't it created in some other way? Is the object universally functional in the way it is for you, or is your purpose for this object or set of objects unique to your experience?

What does it take to create such a thing? What would it take to render it useless? What would it take to utterly destroy it? What would happen in your life experience if it suddenly disappeared?

It may be only a telephone, or a dresser drawer, or your radio dial, or your bathroom mirror, or a lamp shade that you are considering. And yet, all of the questions we might ask about it point out that there is a tremendous complexity that is connected with its existence and its function in your life experience. But, wait! There's more!

If you can, look at it closely. What is it made of? Paper? Plastic? Metal? Wood? Vinyl? Leather? Glass? Granules? Layers? Pages? Dust? Liquid? Solids? Gas? Now look closer. Is it smooth? Slick? Sticky? Rough? Bumpy? Scratchy? Oily? Wet? Dry? Vibrating? Noisy? Big? Small? Long? Short? Dirty?

Now look even closer. What's the smallest component of it you can see with the naked eye? Given the opportunity, what would be the smallest part of it you could see with a magnifying glass? What would you observe with a conventional high-powered microscope? Would you find it alive with creepy, crawly microscopic critters bent on doing you harm?

And if you surveyed it with an electron microscope, what would its dance of molecules look like? Would they be moving fast or slow? What would be their shape? What elements of the chemical table would appear in their makeup? How many protons, neutrons and electrons would be artfully arranged within them?

And what about mesons? And hyperons? And baryons? And quarks? There is a veritable universe of particles, life and motion beyond the scope of your eyes. An actual universe!

Perhaps it is obvious to you that if you had to regard the object of your study in this exercise in terms of the complexity we have explored, it would literally overwhelm you. But you don't have to. It's only a coffee mug, or a telephone, or your reading lamp, or desktop, or whatever it is. And its function for you is cut and dried. You probably don't have to be concerned about its molecular structure. And it is probable that most of the microscopic critters attached to it are harmless.

We exist in time and space somewhere between a universe that is sub-microscopic and one that is super-telescopic. It is a world of "simplexity" let us say. The closer we get to either extreme, the more complicated and confusing things can become. But given the right perspective, we can find a way to view the most complex entities in a simple way just as we can view the simplest things in a very complex way. It is a matter of choice, of choosing a viewpoint.

Choose the simpler view and wrestle with complexity only when there's no other choice.

NO DIFFERENCE IN THE DARK

What are the odds that someone like Helen Keller could be prejudiced against a particular group of people? I think the chances of that would be pretty remote for <u>most</u> if not <u>all</u> people who are born deaf and blind.

For one thing, someone would have to work pretty hard to indoctrinate such a person with enough stereotypes to fertilize a bonafide prejudice. And then I suspect that our subject would have to work fairly diligently on his or her own to <u>maintain</u> the intolerance. After all, many of our prejudices are either based on appearances or suppositions and both of these would tend to disappear in the dim isolation created by not being able to see or hear.

This is certainly true of all our <u>sight-based</u> prejudices. For example, if we were all suddenly stricken blind, we would have to depend on some other way to determine a racial or ethnic identity for each person we encountered. Of course, we could depend on our ears in some cases. Culture, heritage, geography and history all have their ways of helping us to determine the verbal differences between an American Southerner, someone from the Northern U.S., an inner-city African American, a naturalized citizen from the Middle East, or a cantina owner for whom Spanish is a first language.

But what if we couldn't hear? How, then, would we nurture our biases? Would we not be left with the challenge of having to make determinations about each person solely based on what they communicate and how they behave? And isn't that closer to what we should be doing anyway?

And what would happen if our minds were incapable of being narrow or closed? What would occur if there were something about us that refused to allow mental cholesterol to accumulate in the arterial pathways of reasonable and tolerant thought? Wouldn't we have to remain open to the possibility of connectedness with everyone?

I'm convinced that there are very few discernible differences in the dark (or in its physical or psychological equivalents.) There are very few noticeable differences in the darkness of silence. There are very few distinguishable differences in the darkness of the final frontier of space that must surely exist in a truly open mind.

There are, however, <u>many</u> recognizable variances in minds crowded with the concrete pillars of rigid misperceptions of truth.

The world we live in has always been diverse and <u>will</u> always be diverse. The challenge now is that increasing numbers of us are encountering diversity more regularly and more intimately than we ever have. It would be wonderful if we could <u>all</u> <u>embrace</u> it; but that's not likely. So…what shall we do in the meantime?

Perhaps those of us who are suitably enlightened about the insanity of blind prejudice can remind others (who apparently don't know) that what we think we see and understand in the light of our perceptions may not be much different than darkness. We might as well be sightless and deaf if we refuse to be confronted with the blinding illumination of an inescapable truth: We are much more alike than we are different.

There is no difference in the dark.

HIGHEST COMMON DENOMINATOR

(GREATEST COMMON GROUND = GREATEST COMMON GOOD)

In math, when we perform functional operations with fractions, we often attempt to discover the lowest common denominator for the ones with which we are concerned in order to complete an equation.

To add 1/3 and 2/4, for example, we can determine that the lowest common denominator is twelve. In this case, an easy way to establish this is to multiply the denominators we already know by each other. Then by following a process most of us learn in grade school, we convert 1/3 into 4/12 and 2/4 into 6/12. The sum of the two is 10/12 and if we want, we can reduce the resulting fraction to 5/6 by dividing its numerator and denominator by the highest number by which they both can be divided without leaving a remainder. In our example, that number is two.

This whole process works nicely for combining fractions. The lowest common denominator in this case is exactly what we need to determine the highest possible good we can do in solving the problems.

In the process of discovering the highest possible good in human relationships, however, the lowest common denominator leaves much to be desired. Instead, we should make our most valiant attempts to discover what might be called the "highest common denominator."

The Webster Dictionary's second definition for the word denominator says that it is a shared characteristic. As people who share a planet, how much good would it do to continue to search for the highest possible number of common or shared characteristics that we have? Do you suspect as I do that the benefits might be immeasurable? Let's explore that.

Perhaps we can assume that the numerator in our hypothetical ratio is "one" (1) because we are each an individual. Or, if you prefer we can assume that the numerator is one because the original meaning for individual is "undivided" which can be interpreted to suggest that we are all connected anyway. Beginning with either assumption, do you suppose we could agree on a common denominator of twelve for the things we have in common? Let's see.

We are all humans alive on the earth, who have the same basic needs of food and water, clothing and shelter, and we all need love. That's three—or more depending on how you count it.

We all have a biological urge to procreate, sincerely want to be the best we can be, usually live our lives without ever realizing our full potential, and tend to want the best for those we love—especially children. If you're still figuratively nodding your head in agreement, our total of shared characteristics is now seven.

Now let's see: We all want to be loved, tend to be Hedonists who seek pleasure and try to avoid pain, but we all experience pain in our lives. We have a powerful instinct for survival, and we all appreciate beauty as we see it.

If we are still on the same philosophical page, we are now up to twelve. And by the way, unlike with fractions, this process does not require the numerator to change when the denominator does. We are still individuals no matter how many characteristics we have in common.

Since we seem to be on a roll here, let's try for twenty-four as our highest common denominator.

As human beings, we want our own beauty to be appreciated; we want to be happy; we want to be successful; we want to be productive; we want to be free; we sincerely want others to be free; we respond positively when we are truly loved; we are curious; we have an enormous capacity to learn; we want to be touched deeply by someone or something; we really want to get what we need without taking from others; and we would never choose to be violent if we fully understood how to avoid it. That would be twenty-four if we still agree; but you may have raised an eyebrow on one or two of these. Nevertheless, let's try for another dozen.

We are all ultimately a mystery to ourselves; we find others equally if not more mysterious; we recognize some power that is greater than us;

we are all attached to someone or something; we have expectations of our experience—sometimes unfair ones; we believe in justice but sometimes feel that we don't get it; we are often blinded by our own perspectives; we believe in reality but don't know what it is; we are all amazed by something; we all have dreams; we are all creative; and we are all selfish to a degree.

Okay, do you and I now agree on a common denominator of thirty-six? Maybe not. So just in case, why don't we throw in a few more to consider.

We all value family at some level; we all have an impulse towards altruism—caring for others; we enjoy music and art; we like to eat, drink and be merry; we all have more questions than we do answers; and we all would like a chance to spend a million dollars on things that matter to us.

That's another half dozen. But these are all my suggestions. Do you have any? Maybe we can get to a hundred, a thousand, ten thousand! Maybe we have more in common than we have differences. Maybe not. But let's keep adding to the list. Shall we?

THE HUMAN CONTINENT

Here's a question for you: "When we consider who and what we are in relation to others, are we islands…or arbitrarily delineated plots on a human continent?" The way we each answer this question says a lot about our relations with people and a lot about whether or not our connections will be successful, productive or fulfilling.

Consider this: If you are a land owner, do you know the exact location of your property line? You may have a fence erected on the edges of your yard; but if it were not there, would you be able to accurately determine where your land ends and your neighbor's begins?

Okay. Maybe you have four of the infamous "spikes" slammed unobtrusively into the ground by land surveyors to mark the corners of your lawn; and you know exactly where they are. But are you certain that the lot described in your deed has been properly surveyed and marked, or could there have been a human error made by the land appraisers?

If you are an apartment dweller, is the width of the hall outside your door the reason why your living room seems so small? And was it intended to be that size in relation to your space? And do you sometimes feel like your neighbors across the span of drywall that separates you are having their party in your family room? Or is it the other way around?

Of course, you probably recognize and accept the boundaries of your space on faith and custom; and that's fine. But if the real truth were known, your fence might be on your neighbor's property; the city's right-of-way may be encroaching on six inches of your front lawn; or your apartment bathroom may be too small because the flat next door has an extra foot of kitchen space that the architects didn't intend.

When we first moved into our current home, the nearest fence on either side of our house was two or more properties away. The upshot of this was that we and our most immediate neighbors were able to essentially share a huge pseudo-communal back yard. Unfortunately, an exploring four-year old and a tendency for one set of neighbors to destructively encroach on our space led us to be the first to spoil that reality. We built a fence.

I miss that huge back yard; and if we could have hand-picked our neighbors at that crucial time, it's possible we would still have it. With hand-picked residents nearby, mutual respect and trust would have preserved a sense of that communal yard that would have been much like all of America was at one time.

We know that early European settlers in the United States disturbed the nomadic, open and holistic lifestyle of the native peoples who then occupied the continent. It was the European notion of owning land and enclosing it with wire, rails or stones that has served to perhaps divide an otherwise unparceled land-mass forever.

As humans, we come into the world with at least two ready-made boundaries: our skins, and the outer edges of our consciousness. The two of these conspire to create a strong perception of our separateness from everything and everyone else. But is this perception reality or illusion? Are we, in fact, really connected and our skins and awarenesses merely representative of flimsy fences that we can ignore or transmute at will?

If you were able to slowly take a rocket ride into outer space from the physical "inner" space where you are at the moment, you would initially (and with an ever-increasing larger view) see the boundaries that enclose your family room, perhaps, or your bedroom, your office, your car, your home, your yard, your campus, your building, your complex, your neighborhood, your city...and eventually your continent. But the farther away you would travel the less you would be able to see of any boundaries until finally you would see none. The world you live in would at that point be represented by a seamless, shining, blue ball of light nestled amid the black backdrop of a star-studded space.

I wonder what it would take for us to take the same rocket ride up from the confines of our perceived humanness. Perhaps we would initially (and in quick succession) see the enclosures that are represented for each of us by a body, a personality, a set of perceptions, a current awareness, a total consciousness, and perhaps by the boundaries of our intimate relationships.

Would we find that the farther away we would travel the less we would be able to see of any boundaries until finally we would see none? The human experience we live in would then, perhaps, be represented by a seamless, shining, colorless ball of BEING nestled in the middle of an uninterrupted fabric of existence.

Perhaps if we changed perspectives from time to time, walked in another's experiential shoes, viewed the world through another's spectacles of perception, we might be able to see that we are not islands of humanity but thinly encompassed properties in an unbroken human continent.

Perhaps if we could see ourselves as connected we would be less likely to intentionally hurt another in the certainty that we would also be hurting ourselves. All it takes is rising above the illusion of the boundaries we currently accept.

NEITHER ISLANDS NOR CITY-STATES BE
(MORE ON SEPARATENESS AND CONNECTEDNESS)

When we consider who and what we are in relation to others, our perception will put us on one side or the other of a growing debate.

Some will insist we are islands unto ourselves. Others will exclaim that it is more accurate to say that we are arbitrarily delineated plots on a human continent. Should we subscribe to either view? Is the truth somewhere between? How would you respond to these questions?

We may come into the world in a body and a consciousness that is all our own, but do these boundaries mean that we are forever doomed to the limitations we suppose they represent? Is our perception of our separateness from everything and everyone else a reality or an illusion?

If we could see ourselves and our world the way physicists describe them, would we feel the same way about our apparent isolation? If we could perceive the unique and incessant atomic and subatomic dances that represent everything in the Universe, would we be able to tell where our dance ends and another begins?

If we could see a graphic representation of the energy of our thoughts, would we allow ourselves to think the ones that might appear gross or ugly? If we could further perceive how our thoughts interact with other thoughts and other things in our world, would we dare to be so cavalier about what we choose to think? Would we risk being as unconscious as we normally are of the impact of our actions? And what about feelings? Would we monitor them more closely?

You may have seen the automobile commercial aired on television that suggests that a butterfly flapping its wings in a jungle half a world away can set off a chain of events that impacts on an individual's life in the big city. If you haven't, you might want to be on the lookout for it if it ever airs again. In the way that TV advertisements often do, this one says a lot in a very short span of time. And though its ostensible purpose is to call attention to a certain automaker's product, it also highlights a principle that is much more valuable.

What we say and do and feel affects the world of which we are a part. Sometimes the repercussions are deafening. Sometimes they are so subtle that a whisper roars by comparison. Either way, we cannot take lightly the influence we wield on our planet and beyond. We would do well to pay greater attention to the energies we exert in the space and time that we occupy.

I believe in our connectedness…with each other, with every living creature, with every inanimate object, with all energies, with the earth, perhaps with every celestial body we can imagine, and with the Creative Force behind it all. You may not share this belief; but I would invite you to entertain it once in a while. Just thinking about the possibility that everything is connected opens our eyes to the connections that are apparent and makes it possible to discover those that are hidden.

In my mind, we are *not* islands; we *choose* to be "city-states" on the human continent; but we *should* be neither. If nothing else, let's at least begin with recognizing the interrelatedness of humanity.

For me, the awareness of our connectedness has been awakened in a variety of ways. Not the least of these is an old song that still rings in my mind and heart from somewhere in my boyhood memory…

> "No man is an island. No man stands alone.
> Each man's joy is joy to me.
> Each man's grief is my own. We need one another;
> so I will defend each man as my brother—each man as my friend."

Amen.

THEORIES OF RELATIVITY

Albert Einstein is one of my heroes. I respect his scientific achievement, but actually, you may know as much or more about his scientific theories. I can state the formula that represents his theory of relativity ($E=MC^2$) and that's about it. What really gets my motor running when it comes to Einstein is his philosophical prowess.

Well, I'm no Einstein; but I've been thinking about my own "Theories of Relativity"—philosophical ones; and they are all expressed the same way: "Everything is relative!"

Theory One says "Everything is relative!" meaning that everything is connected to everything else in some kind (and to some degree) of relationship.

Scientists sometimes refer to a "primordial soup" from which everything on earth is descended. This "soup" is a mix of chemicals, they say, that contain the building blocks for all animate and inanimate things. The chemicals have randomly arranged themselves through the process of evolution and eventually have become a chicken (or an egg), a drop of water, an apple seed, a rose bush, or your greatest grandparents. A more religious perspective puts an Omnipotent God at the center of things; but even there, God is said to have made man from "the dust of the earth," for example.

So, what's the bottom line? It's simply this: no matter who or what we are, we are all made from cosmic Legos. There are subatomic particles of elements at the root of every molecule of existence that are practically indistinguishable from one another. Everything is relative—somehow connected to everything else, made from the same stuff.

Theory Two says "Everything is relative!" meaning that everything has meaning only in relationship to something else.

Consider anything at all that you want to consider and I believe you'll find that in order to define it at all, you have to consider its relationship to something else. If something is small, that is by comparison to something that is not small. If a person is kind, that is measured against some standard of kindness or some continuum between kindness and meanness. If there is good, there must be evil. If life exists, there must be such a thing as death or "non-life." If there is warmth, there must be coldness. Plants can be defined because they differ from things that are not plants. You exist, and (in a sense) "not you" exists also. Everything is relative—defined by how it is related to something else.

Theory Three says "Everything is relative!" meaning that everything is relevant or pertinent or has something to do with everything else.

Everything that exists or occurs in the world is relevant to every other existence or occurrence in the world. If nothing else, each of these things define what is possible. If a rock exists, then it is possible for rocks to exist. If more than one kind of rock exists, then it is possible for that to be true.

If people can die, then it is possible that people will die. If people live then it is possible for people to live; and if people live now, then it is possible that people will always live—or that they won't.

If spontaneous combustion is possible for one thing, it is possible for another. If one celestial body exists, it opens the door for the existence of others. If things can be alike, things can be different. If an idea is born, other ideas can come into existence. The same can be said of people and animals and wars and cartoon characters. If joy can be defined one way, it can be defined another. Everything is relative—meaning that everything is relevant or pertinent to something else.

Hopefully your understanding is relative to my meaning in a way that honors my intentions. If not, perhaps my intentions will be relative to your expression in a way that honors greater clarity. Whatever happens, though, I will try to remember that everything is relative.

THE PROOF IS IN THE PROOF?

Anything can be proven; and anything can be justified. All it takes is for someone to muster apparently creditable evidence and for the intended audience to buy it "lock, stock, and barrel" with little or no regard for the "real" truth. Unfortunately, that happens all the time. I say it's unfortunate because the real truth is often lost while someone's version of it takes center stage. It doesn't matter that one person's proof is another's doubt.

Most politicians know this. If you ever want to see pseudo-truths proven en masse, watch how thousands (maybe even millions) of people flock to the polls to vote for the proponent of the version of truth that's the most palatable for them. The candidates who tell the real truth are largely ignored by everyone, because no one wants to hear it. We all know that a spoonful of sugar makes the medicine go down; but too often, we are getting more sugar than we are medicine. The proof is in the sweetness.

Proponents of drug legalization or drug decriminalization also know this fact. They have arguments that sound quite reasonable...maybe even imperative...at first blush. But one need only to dig a little bit below the surface of most of those arguments to discover that the foundations are infested with termites of fallacy, or precariously supported on the shifting sands of political or personal expediency. The proof is in the audience's apathy or laziness.

Supporters of the rhetoric of hate are also aware of the power of words that seem to ring true. They generalize or extrapolate from the tiniest occurrences or perceptions to the greatest of revisionist histories and skewed philosophies. They pepper their rhetoric with emotionally charged terms that move people ever farther from the truth and ever closer to destruction by their own hatred. For them, the proof is in the camaraderie of their hateful misconceptions. But the bells of their truth are made of glass. Sooner or later, they will shatter under the onslaught of their own incessant and insensitive ringing.

Those who play the various confidence games also know. Whether it's a fly-by-night evangelist; a selfish Don Juan or Lolita; an insurance vulture preying on the weak and vulnerable; or an investment counselor who is motivated by visions of his or her own wealth rather than the client's; there are those who will not hesitate to tell you the truth they want you to believe while concealing the view of the way things really are. The proof is in the once devout, now cynical believers. The proof is in the tear-stained faces of the broken-hearted who were persuaded to love an empty shell. The proof is in the elder who invests a life's savings in a bottomless financial pit that never delivers the promised comfortable retirement.

Anything can be proven, and anything can be justified…unless we insist on always seeking the truth. We should all pretend to be from Missouri, the "Show-Me State." We might then accept nothing as truth unless we have overwhelming empirical evidence that can hardly be contradicted. Any speaker of the truth would have to <u>show</u> us that what they speak is true.

Then again, that might be a little dangerous. After all, there are some things we have to accept without tangible proof or we can't accept them at all. Belief in God is one outstanding example. Belief in baby pigeons is another. Think about it. Have <u>you</u> ever <u>seen</u> one?

But even when material proof is not possible, there is such a thing as a conscience, a gut-level feeling, an intuition, a hunch, an "I don't know how I know it; I just know it!" kind of belief that brings us the truth more often than we might think. But to trust that voice, we have to be able to do something that frightens most of us; we must <u>know</u> and <u>love</u> and <u>trust</u> our selves. If it were easy to do, we'd all be doing it and be better off. It's NOT easy; but the peace of mind and the unwavering and unassailable courage of our convictions are well worth the effort.

Anything can be proven; anything can be justified. But remember; no one can lead us down the primrose path without our consent. Consent only to "the <u>truth</u>, the <u>whole</u> truth and <u>nothing but</u> the truth."

A PARADIGM FOR LIFE
(TESTING CRITICAL PERCEPTIONS)

What follows is a test. There are only three questions. The format is true or false, but there may be no right or wrong answers. Yet, in order for anyone (and every_one) to do well on the FINAL EXAM, there's only one possible answer for each question on this test and we all have to choose it.

If enough of us choose the alternative answer, we will, by doing so, guarantee a failing grade on the FINAL EXAM for ourselves and probably for everyone else. Confused? Well, wait until you see the statements you must evaluate.

1. There are enough resources in the world for all people to have what they need and much of what they want.
2. Every person in the world is entitled to have all of his or her needs fulfilled and many desires satisfied.
3. In places where resources seem scarce, people have the power to either find and acquire resources that have been overlooked, to migrate to locations where resources are more available, or to compel resources to come to them.

That's the end of the test. Now, you get to grade it. Here's how you determine your score.

For question #1, if you chose TRUE as your answer, then you view our world as one of abundance rather than scarcity. You believe that when a person does not have access to basic necessities and at least a modicum of hearts desires, it has nothing to do with whether or not they are available on earth. In fact, you are certain they are available. You also know this to be perpetually true regardless of how many people live on the earth, what needs they may have, or how many reasonable desires they are able to gratify.

If you chose FALSE as your answer for question #1, you see the earth as a world of scarcity rather than abundance. You believe that there are limited resources available and that when a certain number of people are able to acquire them, certain other people will necessarily have to do without. You are, therefore, also inclined to believe in axioms such as "first come, first served," "every man for himself," and "survival of the fittest."

Furthermore, if you are a selfish person, then you are determined to get yours regardless of whether others get theirs or not. If you are a selfless person, then you have probably decided that you must sacrifice your own needs and desires so that those you care about will thrive.

If you answered TRUE for question #2, you are among those people who will not justify your acquisitions by asserting that you are somehow more deserving of your just rewards than certain others. Instead, you know and understand that anyone who is alive on the earth (or who has ever been) has as much right to the riches of the earth as anyone else.

If FALSE was your answer to question #2, then your belief is that some people are more deserving of an appropriate share of earth's treasures than others. You are then left with the need to decide which of the earth's population will be the HAVES and which will be the HAVE NOTS. Obviously, you will do everything in your power to be sure that you are among the HAVES. Then, of course, once your status is secure, you will (depending on the level of generosity in your heart) choose either to dole out a pittance (or more) to the HAVE NOTS, or you will simply remove yourself from any concern about them at all.

Question #3 is obviously the most provocative (and perhaps the most difficult) of the three. But if TRUE was the choice you made, then you wholeheartedly believe in the power of the individual to somehow acquire those things which satisfy needs and relevant wants. You know that people will either find what they need where they are, go to where they can find it, or summon resources to themselves through communication, prayer, or perhaps the sheer force of their will.

A response of FALSE means that apparent scarcity of resources is cause for hopelessness, helplessness, despair and defeat as far as you're concerned. If you (or someone else) are doomed to the world of the HAVE NOTS, you see no point in digging the extra foot, walking the extra mile, or trying for the thousandth time. You believe there comes a time when no amount of effort will bring forth fruit. You believe too many things are impossible.

The FINAL EXAM measures whether or not we are each able to achieve the needs and desires that are appropriate for us before we die. If we do, we pass the FINAL; if we don't, we fail.

The class we are taking is LIFE 101; we are all in it; and a satisfactory performance on the test you have just taken is a prerequisite for how well the whole class performs on the FINAL. It's graded on a special curve.

You are welcome to change your answers before you decide what your grade is on this test. But remember; the final evaluation for all of us may depend on how you respond.

THE PARADIGM OF JIGSAW PUZZLES
(FITTING OURSELVES TO OUR WORLDVIEW)

With almost no exceptions, my whole family of origin loved jigsaw puzzles. My dad thought jigsaw puzzle construction was mostly a spectator sport; but even he was known to plunk in a piece occasionally when a pile of those tiny little cardboard fragments showed up in his house.

But there can be no question about the rest of us. At one time, there were at least three generations of jigsaw lovers in my family that would go slightly bonkers at the sight of those interlocking pieces of cardboard.

Apart from the fact that we would find them a really fun way to enjoy some family togetherness, maybe we also intuitively connected with how much jigsaw puzzles reflect qualities of living itself.

For the uninitiated (although I can't imagine that there are any) jigsaws usually come in a box that illustrates a scene or design on its cover that is what the finished puzzle should look like. There are some novelty puzzles which are blank, a single color, or a repetitive pattern; but most puzzles allow you to start with a vision of your goal. That's very helpful.

With the vision constantly before you, you can accurately measure your progress as you move toward the goal. You can also identify important elements of the vision that can be worked on separately and maybe even by different people as the pieces are carefully put into place. The vision keeps you (and others) from aimlessly wandering or curiously wondering.

All jigsaws have a framework, a perimeter, a border—and most people construct that first. When you know what your parameters are, you can be much more focused in your approach toward functioning within them.

Most jigsaws have uniquely shaped pieces that fit within the puzzle in a singular way. Some novelty puzzles have pieces that are identically shaped but they still have exclusive functions in the construction of the whole. When you can determine how certain pieces fit, it reduces the number of existing pieces which have no apparent function in the process. Yet at the same time, you know that if they are available, they must fit somehow and somewhere.

Sometimes two or more puzzle pieces will be so similar in construction and appearance that they are almost…almost interchangeable. But when a piece is a perfect fit, you know it. You know in every way possible that the fit is correct. It practically jumps into place as if no effort was required to fit it at all. And yet, your glee is increased because you also know that a great deal of effort may have been expended to discover and correctly orient the matching pieces for the joining!

Most jigsaws allow for a certain amount of categorizing of elements. There may be mostly blue sky pieces, or mostly green tree pieces, or mostly brown boat pieces, or mostly multi-colored flower pieces, or mostly striped, streaked, dotted or two-toned pieces. Identifying categories for elements of the puzzle reduces the amount of chaos that can overwhelm you when you begin.

Some puzzles are printed on both sides. That can certainly add to the confusion and chaos. But most puzzles have a blank or dark side that reduces by half the number of separate bits of information you have to consider. When you can eliminate the dark side, your task is much easier.

Probably the greatest single frustration for jigsaw lovers is to lose a piece of the puzzle. There may be 2,000 fragments successfully reconstructed; but if a single piece is missing, there is weeping and wailing and gnashing of teeth. But if the errant cornerstone is unearthed, the joy in Jigsaw Camelot is unbounded!

There are people who enjoy the challenge of novelty puzzles but usually only after they have had quite a bit of experience with conventional ones. For those who are tackling unconventional puzzles for the first time, it's good to have the insight of those who have treaded on those grounds before.

With jigsaw puzzles and human lives, strategies for success are much the same. Normally, it is helpful to take a hands-on approach. Always keep the vision before you and allow it to guide you toward a purpose. Allow and encourage others to help you because it's easier and more fun. Know what your parameters are and then recognize and purposefully employ all of the unique elements available which can help you maximize the possibilities. Reduce chaos by categorizing elements where appropriate; but never force a fit where one is not intended. Use the dark side to help you know what deserves your attention. Never rest until you've done your best to fulfill the purpose. And be sure to thoroughly celebrate all of your successes.

MY BROTHERS

Sometimes my brothers
Are the ones whose mothers
Are not my own.

Sometimes I wonder
If, in fact, there can be
A "spirit clone".

There can be kinship
Among perfect strangers
When psyches meet.

Often the meeting
Can create new soul mates
Who grow complete.

I look for brothers
When I'm touching others
With my heart strings.

When their vibrations
Echo softly in me,
My heart just sings!

A contradiction
Might appear most likely
When brothers are...

Completely female.
But they're still my……………...siblings.
(All people are.)

PEOPLE ARE LIKE CLOUDS

People are like clouds. And maybe there's a lesson for us in that.

People come in all shapes and sizes, types and colors. They exist all over the world. Sometimes they're born in one place but most of their lives may be spent somewhere else. The substance of them comes from the earth, but the power that gives them life comes from beyond the earth, an invisible force called soul or spirit. People are important, but not more important than the earth from which they come.

Now, consider clouds. Their types include those which we call by names like cirrus, cumulus, cirrocumulus, nimbus, cumulonimbus, or thunderhead, funnel, wall and so on. Their colors can appear to be white, yellow, orange, red, violet, blue, green, gray, brown or black; yet, they are all made of water... which is colorless and transparent.

Clouds may form over the ocean and spend most of their lives in the mountains, or be born in the mountains and live in several places between the oceans before they expire. The water from which they are made covers most of the earth, but they wouldn't even exist if it were not for the sun which calls to them from the heavens. And, of course, they can be important to the earth but not more important than the earth. Hmmmmmmmm....

Clouds come from the earth and return to the earth. (Sounds like "ashes to ashes and dust to dust" to me.) Clouds are born inauspiciously, gradually grow, and exist for a certain—perhaps preordained—amount of time (which can differ markedly from the life-span of others.) Then, when they reach their fullest maturity, they make a transition and cease to exist as clouds. They become some form of precipitation and.... well, we know the rest. Or do we?

Is that the end for clouds? Or is it possible that the same microscopic droplets of water gather again to form a new cloud? Maybe only some of the same cloud vapors return and thus are born sons and daughters of their parent clouds.

People are what they are. But, in a way, they are also how we imagine them. When they see themselves, they probably have self-concepts much different than the notions we have of them. Sometimes, they are secretive. They hide things. But at other times, they open windows that allow us to see more of them, or even things that are greater than they are.

But, what about clouds? They are what they are, but they are also how we imagine them: *"Oh look, Tony! That one looks like a clown with a big, bald head!" "Yeah, Cindy, that's almost as cool as the 'Bugs Bunny Eating A Carrot' we saw a little while ago!"*

We make of clouds whatever we imagine them to be; and yet, they must ultimately be true to their ever-changing selves—not true to our expectations. Wouldn't it be wonderful if we could remember that about people?!!!

Clouds can hide things, too—other clouds, hail, dangerous storms, the sun, the moon, planets, comets, stars, aircraft. But they can also open to reveal any or all of the above—and more. They can even focus a beam of sun right on top of a grassy hill, or on a stately tree in the middle of a gloomy forest. And when we can witness such a serendipitous display, don't we sort of feel like it was meant just for us?

If we were to learn from what might be considered the best in clouds, perhaps this is what we would do: We would discover our lives somewhere, rise up to a level for growth that seems right for us, and grow to our fullest potential. Along the way, we would try to create as much beauty as possible and experience a full spectrum of colorful possibilities.

Perhaps we would travel where the winds of destiny would take us, but we'd be sure to catch only the currents of purpose, the breezes of reason, the gales of greatness, and the jet-streams of dreams.

We would keep nothing of importance hidden from others or ourselves, and we would reveal everything that deserves notice. We would inspire imagination in others, but never take for granted that others are what we imagine them to be.

We would treat earth like a loving mother and take only that which is necessary for our existence and growth while working to repay and replenish her with the significance of our lives. We would treat the other great force that calls us into being like a loving father and live lives that justify the summons.

And perhaps when we ceased to exist as the entities we had come to know, we would continue to live anyway through the people we touch, the monuments we help to create, the sons and daughters who are born to us, or (Who knows?) perhaps even in ways that we have not yet envisioned!

IT IS NOT "IT"
(DETERMINING OUR VIEW OF OTHERS)

Martin Buber was right. When we consider the "others" that are in our world, it's important to regard them in the same light that we regard ourselves. If we value the "I", we must also value the "Thous." In relationships of all kinds, we must know the difference between "I/Thou" and I/It."

It is too often true that we see each other as objects rather than as persons. As a result, we <u>treat</u> persons <u>as</u> objects. They become the objects of our affections, or the objects of our hatred, or the objects of our fears, our anger, or our adoration. It can go on and on...and usually does. We would do better to consider them the <u>subjects</u> of our thoughts, feelings and actions.

When we objectify someone, we completely externalize them. We may go so far as to consider them <u>utterly</u> and <u>irrevocably</u> separate from us. They might as well be rocks, or trees, or items of garbage. It can easily go to that extent and often does. When we <u>sub</u>jectify someone, what we do instead is to recognize the substance of being human. This is far different from valuing only the qualities or attributes that a person has which may engender our admiration, or loathing, or anything between.

In one <u>philosophical</u> context, the word "subject" is taken to mean "the mind or ego that thinks and feels, as distinguished from everything outside the mind." So say my good buddies Noah Webster and company.

<u>People</u> <u>think</u> and <u>feel</u>! Rocks do neither. Go ahead; crush a rock if you want. That may suit an important purpose for you; and you can be fairly certain that the rock will have no thoughts or feelings about it—one way, or another. But don't crush people. They are not rocks.

People think and feel. Bicycles do neither. You can own a bicycle. You can also ride it until it falls apart and then go get another. The bike you discard will not be emotionally or psychologically affected by your choice. You cannot own people, however. You may control them; or they may allow you to treat them as if you own them rather than risk a greater evil of discomfort, or pain, or violence, or death (at an extreme.) But you can never really own them. And if you plan to ride them until they fall apart, they cannot so easily be replaced. Their functions can be replaced, but they are irreplaceable. And they will always have thoughts and feelings that will be reflected back toward you—probably in a negative way.

People think and feel. A piece of wood does neither. You may shape, mold, or manipulate a piece of wood in order to accomplish a number of different purposes and then perhaps even reuse, recycle or reshape it for even more purposes until it might no longer be recognizable as wood. The wood will never complain, never suffer, never feel put upon, and never think ill of you for your choices. A person may ultimately be as malleable as a piece of wood but she or he is not wood and should not be treated as if they were.

I will not argue that you probably already know this very clearly. But I will ask you to consider two questions: (1) If you already know these things, do your actions always reflect the knowing? and (2) If your actions match your awareness, can you say the same for the rest of the world?

In my mind, we would have fewer runaway children if they were treated more like people and less like property. The same is true for husbands or wives who accept divorce rather than a marriage where they are objectified. They may, indeed, simply be choosing the lesser of two evils.

We would certainly have fewer thefts, burglaries, assaults, murders and wars if we could clearly see the humanity of our victims. But it is often not their humanity we see. We can't see the subject because we are too busy looking at the object.

Martin Buber was right.

WHOSE SHOW IS THIS ANYWAY?
(OR "YOU DON'T HAVE TO BE A STAR IN MY SHOW")

Have you ever been in a movie or a stage show? If you haven't, have you ever fantasized about being in one? If you can answer yes to either of these questions, I suspect you are like a lot of other people. Many of us have appeared in some sort of production whether it was a kindergarten play, an amateur video, a high school or college musical, community theater, merely "The Cinema Of The Mind," or a bonafide Hollywood or Broadway project.

You may have had a major part, a leading role, or even star billing in the shows of which you have been a part. I would be willing to bet, though, that whatever part you played was ultimately one of your choosing. Even if it wasn't a plum role, I suspect that in the final analysis, you gave your consent to becoming the character you interpreted. You wouldn't have had it any other way, right? Right!!

But, would you say the same thing about the roles you play everyday? I mean, do you really choose them all? Are you the producer and director of your personal daily soap opera? Or is the drama you live everyday the brainchild of one or more of the other people in your life?

Do you keep getting thrust into roles that really don't fit you? Do other people type-cast you in ways that are foreign to how you see yourself? Is someone else forcing you to star in a show that they feel they can see and understand but which is completely invisible to you?

You might be surprised to know that without your awareness or knowledge, there may be many "productions" in which you are starring or have a pivotal role. Of course, it doesn't really matter that you are oblivious to this fact until the reviews come out; but at that point, you will either be in for some pleasant surprises (if you're lucky) or you're going to get raked over the coals! I'll give you three guesses as to which is more likely.

You see, someone may have you cast as a hero or heroine. They worship the ground you <u>would</u> be walking on if you were a mere mortal. They expect miracles from you on a regular basis. In their eyes you can do no wrong. Their well-being is somehow inextricably connected to you. The climate of both their inner and outer worlds is regulated by your mere presence. The sun rises for them in your smile. They would happily gather your tears like rain drops to nurture the guilt they would feel in the certainty that they had somehow caused them.

Hey, that's not such a bad role…until you trip and fall, screw up on a miracle, make a mistake, admit a shortcoming, or ad-lib within your assigned role in some way that they do not expect or can't understand. At that point, you are deep in "Uh-Oh Land."

Someone else (or sometimes even the same persons) may cast you as a villain. In this role, nothing you do is right. As a performer, you are constantly being criticized for what you do and how you do it, and you get to be the bad guy or the tramp even when you're trying your best to be good. When you speak your lines, you get accused of saying the wrong things when you are certain you said exactly what was needed for your role as you understand it. Sometimes you even get blamed for thinking things that you are not, or intending things that are not even in your awareness! In this role, you get plenty of on-going negative feedback from your director (or directors); but then critics add injury to insult and the next thing you know, people who may be perfect strangers are booing and hissing at you and you have no idea why.

There are also other roles you may get to play sometimes when you may not have an inkling that you're even in a show. The Village Idiot, The Victim, The Slave, The Soldier, The Deaf/Mute, The Scapegoat, The Clown, The Counselor, The Police Officer, The Garbage Collector. There are tons of roles in which you may be cast by a friend, an acquaintance, a loved one, an employer, or an enemy…without your consent, and quite often without your knowledge. But, guess what: you may very well be casting others in unwanted roles, too!

But, all is not lost. Knowing that these kinds of creations are being produced is half the battle. The other half is remembering that there is always a producer/director and you have as much (actually more) of a right to be <u>that</u> person as anyone does. After all, you're the star of the show and your contract says you can exercise creative control.

If you're going to appear or star in this kind of show, make sure you retain creative control. If you relinquish that to someone else—willingly or not—you are also pretty much letting go of any possibility of influencing the outcome of critical reviews. And we all know that the reviews can make you or break you.

I don't know about you, but I want to be sure that the critics only get to judge my performance in roles that I choose myself—not those that are projected on to me by someone else.

FROM THE DIRECTOR'S CHAIR
(HELP FOR FINDING MORE INSIDE)

In my capacities as a performer, a writer and a teacher, I have from time to time taken direction from someone else. Sometimes it comes by choice; at other times, it's because it comes with the territory.

As a teacher, I have responded to the administration of principals. As a writer, I have been subject to input from editors. As an actor, I have had to take direction from directors. As an independent performer, I have learned to carefully monitor the reactions from my audiences and clients, and to also formally and informally survey them for feedback. The end result—in almost every case—is a sharpening of my skills in these various areas.

In some ways, logic might suggest that we are always in the best position to observe ourselves and to know what talents, abilities and passions lurk within. Yet any of us who have been conscious enough of our relationships with caring, thoughtful and observant people (who also supervise us in some way) have probably learned otherwise. The first of these lessons for many of us very likely came from parents or grandparents.

Sometimes others can see in us what we might never discover in ourselves. They can draw out of us what we might never have imagined was in us. All it takes for us to benefit from this conception is the advantage of understanding the different perspective, and a willingness to look at ourselves from that viewpoint.

The first half of this dynamic is often very easy to come by. There is usually no shortage of people who are willing to give us an opinion about something we choose to be or something we choose to do. It's the second component that is frequently much harder. Because the opinions of others are often perceived as negative or destructive criticism (even when they are not), our willingness to view ourselves through the eyes of others is often sorely lacking.

But we need not give up hope. We can still take advantage of a constructive view from the director's chair, so to speak, and there are at least two ways we can do it.

Perhaps one of the best initiatives we can take to uncover hidden greatness in ourselves is to simply ask for the help of people we trust. Maybe they can privately share candid views about certain personal aspects we hope to enrich. We might also openly ask for perspectives of their choosing about spheres in our lives that they believe we could make better. Either way, we can sometimes get a vision of ourselves that is significantly different from our own.

An alternative to this kind of help from a friend is to be openly, affirmatively, intuitively and tenaciously self-evaluative. In other words, we have to regularly take a good, hard look at who we are, what we do, and how we do it and make valiant attempts to be ever better.

This is much more difficult, however, because we have trouble being open, self-affirming, intuitive and resolute in our self-appraisal while also being honest. As often as not for some of us, it is more like self-flagellation. We beat ourselves up in a way that makes us livid when others do it.

Finally, it is left to us to find a way to benefit from the insights of others into ourselves. Diamonds cannot cut and polish themselves. They need the help of designers who can see hidden beauty beneath a dull and crusty exterior. So, I think, do we.

THE BRILLIANT SERVER
(BRENDA AND THE BEST OF THE REST)

'd like to have you join me in celebrating "The Brilliant Server"; and I think I'd like to dedicate the celebration to Brenda. Brenda was part of the nursing team which cared for my mother after a major surgery. She epitomizes what we are celebrating.

I had the pleasure of getting to know Brenda while she was on duty. She worked on the two days I could visit my Mom who was recuperating in a rehabilitation hospital in my home town.

Brenda reminded me once again of how special it is to be served by someone who apparently considers work a joy rather than a job, a privilege rather than a mere responsibility, an opportunity rather than an inconvenience.

Brenda is beautiful. Part of what makes her that way is a smile so warm that ice probably melts more quickly in its presence. She also has a quick laugh that reaches the ears and the heart like happy music while lighting her eyes and whatever room she happens to be in.

Brenda is loving. She is the kind of nurse who is likely to get marriage proposals from male patients who are looking for real love in their lives and who miss (or ignore) the fact that she's already married. Shy little ones might easily wind up going for a tour, or a snack, cuddled in her arms or walking along in the tow of one of her strong and gentle hands. Senior citizens might feel her presence and her caring as if she were a daughter rather than a nurse—maybe even more so than with their real daughters and sons. Sometimes children do little more than tolerate elderly parents in their infirmity.

If Brenda were nothing more, she would still be a cut above many who work to serve the public. But Brenda is also wise, and courageous, and strong, and thoughtful, and principled, and honest, and open, and friendly, and joyful, and dedicated, and a lot of things you would expect or hope for public servants to be. Unfortunately, far too many of them are not. But Brenda is; and it seems to show in whatever she does.

Instead of Brendas, we often get "Brats" of all ages who are arrogant, ignorant, apathetic, indifferent, surly, cowardly, narrow-minded, thoughtless, unscrupulous, shallow, opaque, unhappy, and/or dedicated only to themselves. You know the ones I mean. You see them everywhere.

One of these people might show up as the 16-year-old clerk at your favorite discount department store who doesn't smile, who begrudgingly greets you—if at all—and who speaks with a disembodied monotone that tells you in an instant that what's really discounted is you. You don't matter except as a means to their end of receiving a paycheck.

Some of these people appear as attendants in full-service gas stations. They less- than-efficiently check and adjust your car's fluid levels and seem put out when you point out that checking the tire pressure or tranny fluid would be nice too. They rip off your charge receipt, or plop down your change, and mumble "thank you" (if you're lucky); and you leave wondering if they are really human or just prototypical, space-age androids.

Reluctant servers show up in hotels and restaurants and at airline ticket counters. They hang out in fast food joints, souvenir shops, amusement parks and garages. They drive taxis and delivery trucks. They wash cars and teach children. Some are even ministers, lawyers, counselors, and health care professionals. They are all over; and in my mind, they have only two redeeming qualities: they are at least somewhat functional, and they make the Brendas of the world seem even more marvelous.

Fortunately, there are lots of Brendas around, too. Maybe there aren't as many as we would like to see, but they're there and they need to be affirmed. They need to know we appreciate that for them the word "job" might be spelled with the letters "J-O-Y."

Thank goodness for the Brendas of the world. They are the ones who make us feel at home…or at least in a place that feels like home ought to be. They can make you smile—sometimes even when you don't feel like it. They can make you feel loved or cared for in addition to being served. You seldom are aware when they are having a bad day—even if they have many—and they can even take most jerks in stride. In short, they are the ones who always get heartfelt recognition from me whether it's in the form of a thoughtful comment, a generous tip, a personal note, or perhaps all three.

You should find a way to affirm brilliant servers. Of course, I wouldn't ask you to do something that I wouldn't do myself. So in case, you need a little inspiration to go the extra mile, I offer this set of limericks that a brilliant server got from me a few years ago. I like to think that she still has the napkin I wrote it on tucked in a scrap book somewhere. I know I would still have it.

Babs of Quality Inn

At Quality Inn, there is "Babs".
She's the one who "picks up tabs"—
Not because she is rich,
But because of her niche
As the manager. She also "gabs".

She "gabs" because she's kind of nice,
With a smile that can surely melt ice!
Just because she has style,
She shared fun with me while
I was stranded. Plus dinner! (Same price.)

For the people who give extra "stuff"
With the service, a tip's not enough.
So, for her, here's a rhyme
Just for that special time;
Though it's one that was penned "off the cuff."

Hey, not bad for the lull between dinner and the end of dessert!
Can there ever be too much said about servers who reach for excellence in what they do and in who they are?

MORE ON THE BRILLIANT SERVER
(WHEN PUBLIC SERVICE IS A JOY)

When I think about Brenda and Babs and other Brilliant Servers, it really gets me thinking about people who work to serve the public in some capacity. I often wonder how some people who work as clerks, and secretaries, and nurses, and waiters, and various other attendants ever get their jobs in the first place.

I'd like to think it comes from managerial desperation rather than oversight or indifference. But, who knows. All I know is I value excellence in service when I see it and if I were a manager, there are some people who could never work for any length of time under my supervision.

Years ago, I visited a Pizza Hut where my sister Paula worked part-time for a while. She was then (and is now) the kind of person I would hire if I were an employer and compliment or tip generously if I were a customer that she served.

On a particularly busy evening, I watched her darting around from serving bar to dining tables to entrances serving pizza, busing tables and seating customers. My appearance was a surprise because I was standing in for my Dad who was scheduled to pick her up. When she spotted me, she acknowledged me with a big smile and a big, bright "Hey!" that befitted a brother/sister relationship that is also a best-friendship. But at the same time, she couldn't break her flow for a hug or a momentary visit.

"Just a minute," she said, "I'll be right back." She flitted around a bit more attending to various duties, joked with co-workers, warmly greeted new customers and assured them she'd be right with them (which she was.) Simultaneously, she checked on other diners, and never missed a beat or a smile.

"What's up?" she asked me when she could get me back into her busy flow. "I'd like some pizza," I answered. "Oh!" she said, genuinely surprised that I came to eat. "In that case, right this way, sir," she said with mock earnestness.

She got me seated, took my order, and visited for a bit; then she was off to attend to the needs of her other customers before her shift ended and I took her home. She was a joy to watch. My sister, who now teaches children, is a brilliant server.

Speaking of teachers, I know some in my home town and elsewhere who are also brilliant servers. One in particular comes to mind at the moment. Her name is Terry and she teaches at the primary level in an elementary school.

Terry came to the education profession later than many do and has not been at it very long; but somebody needs to be sure that she sticks around for as long as is humanly possible. She is a wonderful teacher!

I have watched her work in her classroom and been amazed at her rapport, her caring, her control, and the respect she gets from her students, their parents and her colleagues. But when you see what she does and how she does it, it's no wonder that she's so effective and respected.

Terry loves her students and treats them all as if they were her own children. That much is obvious. Not only does she teach them their grade-level curriculum, but her classroom is also a laboratory for learning about life. I don't think she would miss a teachable moment if it were trying to hide from her. She doesn't just teach. She listens; she learns with her students; she is genuinely interested in who they are and what they can become; she empowers them; she inspires them. She is a brilliant server.

I really want to encourage you to acknowledge and affirm the brilliant server wherever you find one. They deserve all the accolades they can get. Take a little extra time to call attention to specifics about a server that you value—efficiency, caring, congeniality, timeliness, conversation, genuine interest in you or others, attention to detail, or whatever other ways they go above the call of duty.

Write them a note or even a little poem. Keep nice little trinket gifts handy and give them to attendants who don't get tipped or as an added bonus for those who do. Make a phone call from time to time to your kids' teachers who are wonderful, and just tell them "Thanks." I suspect that such affirmations will be as meaningful as (or perhaps more meaningful than) anything else you could do.

If you are in a position that allows you to hire people who serve others, train them to be brilliant on the job. Better yet, hire mostly the ones who give indications during the interview that they will be brilliant if you give them a chance. You must never forget that they are on the front lines of your campaign for success and customer satisfaction.

If servers in your employ can't be brilliant (or at least bright) send them to look for a job where it doesn't matter if they are or not. If they wind up working for your competition, that's to your advantage anyway. But don't forget to treat all of your employees with dignity and respect and try your best to somehow pay the great ones what they're worth. Sometimes, all it takes are kind words genuinely and generously shared.

INHUMANITY
(WHAT IS THE STANDARD FOR MEASUREMENT?)

'd like to think that anything less than treating others as we want to be treated is inhuman. But with that criterion, so many humans are currently guilty of "inhumanity" that we would obviously need to rethink our standards for what it means to be human. But what would the standards really be?

In the Star Trek story archives, humans are always being "dissed" (as some slang users might say to mean "disrespected") by one galactic species or another. If it's not the Klingons disrespecting humankind, it's the Romulans. If it's not "Q" and the beings of The Continuum treating people like nursery school playthings, it's the machine-like Borg attempting to wipe them from existence in the Universe. Even the particularly hideous and less than honorable Ferengi look down their considerable noses in disdain and sneer at the creatures they call "HUE—mons."

Now if you're not into Star Trek, these references may not mean a lot to you. But suffice it to say that the story lines are often created in such a way that human beings are judged by other creatures according to the most evil and disheartening choices we've made over the course of our history. In other words, humans are considered the senseless creatures that are capable of incredibly destructive wars, hideous crimes, genocide, and the poisoning of the planet—not to mention some of the lesser evils.

Fortunately, 24th Century earth in Star Trek is a shining example of the ability of earth's inhabitants to rise above their faults to a level where a much more sensible (perhaps even near-perfect) human society exists. UNfortunately, that is just the vision of the late Gene Roddenberry and company. As we go spiraling into the 21st Century, it sometimes seems more like the spiral that leads to the sewer than the one that sends the Olympic discus or hammer into flight. We are still very much the creatures who are capable of incredibly destructive wars, hideous crimes, genocide, the poisoning of the planet and a whole host of lesser evils.

My family missed the big screen version of the movie Schindler's List but found it nonetheless impactful when we cracked the seal on a video-taped copy that is now a part of our home library. We watched it over the course of two evenings at home.

As usual, Stephen Spielberg did a masterful job of creating a riveting, cinematic vision of something that can too easily fade from awareness and memory. But for me, there's an even greater horror than the Holocaust of World War II, and the American orgies of destruction represented by the so-called Indian Wars, and the horrifying institution of slavery. These destroyed the lives of countless North American Natives, Africans and African-Americans.

For me, the greater horror is that today, there are people around the world who would actually like to see such dark chapters of world history repeated. Who could have imagined that the conflicts in Bosnia would have brought so-called "ethnic cleansing" barely fifty years after and in a geographical area very close to where the world was made to swallow the same bitter pill by German Nazis under another name—The Final Solution.

Who could have conceived that we would (once again) see the day when churches in African American communities would be torched by hateful people? Who could have fathomed the kind of fear and loathing that would take the lives of nearly two hundred innocent people in an act of domestic terrorism in Oklahoma City? How could we have anticipated the countless people world-wide who are still made to suffer because somebody thinks it makes sense?

Somehow, we must keep striving to reach the ideal for humanity that makes the term "inhumanity" actually mean something. Perhaps we can start by refusing to allow anything inhuman to get a toehold in our collective psyche. Please speak out for tolerance, Truth (with a capital "T"), and Love. And, for humanity's sake, speak vehemently against anything less.

A CASE FOR THE GOLDEN RULE
(ANOTHER NOTE ON HUMAN INHUMANITY)

I got my feelings hurt not long ago. That's not the first time, and it probably won't be the last; but I don't mention it so we can have a little "Pity Party" and exclaim, "Oh, ain't it awful!" Instead I want to point out what may be at the root of why it occurred.

The details of the circumstance are not important. Let's just say that a couple of people reacted to me in a way that was intentionally hurtful. Let's also say that if the shoe had been on the other foot, I would absolutely not have done the same thing. And I don't make this statement because I'm in need of your applause. Instead, I just want us to think for a moment about an ages-old axiom that is embedded in some, while it is little more than an exercise in meaningless rhetoric for others.

What I refer to is a statement that many of us refer to as the "Golden Rule." In simple language, it dictates that we should treat others the way we want to be treated. Some of us learned it in the very poetic form of the King James Bible where the words are, "Do unto others as you would have them do unto you."

It is a simple admonition, but the power inherent in it escapes far too many of us. We almost always want it to apply to us if we are on the receiving end of what is done, but we are sometimes not very strong advocates when we are the ones who are doing.

I am one who tries to keep this rule in mind at all times when dealing with people. I never want to be responsible for treating someone else in a way that I would not want to be treated. And when my human imperfection is responsible for some misdeed along these lines, I try to apologize and make amends if at all possible. And where it may not be possible, I am more than a little bit remorseful. I find it very difficult to apply the idea of "forgive and forget" to myself. An ever-present seed of memory almost always remains to remind me not to repeat the behavior; and though I can accept my imperfections, a kernel of anguish remains to keep me in touch with the emotional cost of harm.

I really like the phrase in the Hippocratic Oath of the medical world that says, "I will do no harm." That is my intention in every moment of my life. I just wish it were as easy to accomplish as it is to intend.

But what <u>really</u> troubles me is that as difficult as it is for <u>me</u> to live by the Golden Rule, it must be even <u>more</u> difficult for a lot of other people. I place this value of benevolent reciprocity as one of my very highest and still, I falter. What about people who prefer the motto of "Do unto others <u>before</u> they do unto you?" What chance do <u>they</u> have of not hurting others? And what about people who think being hurt by others is <u>normal</u> and <u>acceptable</u>? Their commandment might be more like, "Do unto others <u>as</u> they do unto you."

I suppose our greatest hope is that those of us who work diligently to abide by this Golden Rule will continue to hang on to it in the face of all opposition. I think we <u>must.</u>

Those of us who value ourselves and others being always treated with dignity and respect must never stoop to a level where "turnabout is fair play." We must never lose sight of the fact that "an eye for an eye and a tooth for a tooth" will eventually make us all blind and the owners of dentures. And where is the justice in that? Or perhaps that <u>is</u> justice for choosing not to abide by the Rule.

NEW YEARS, NEW LIVES, NEW VIEWS, AND OTHER CELEBRATIONS

STRANGER'S EYES

I love to see
With Stranger's Eyes.
What's common holds
A new surprise
When viewed as though
It hasn't been
So often heard
Or felt or seen.

A street that's near
My neighborhood
Is lined with trees
That look so good
When Spring has come
And green leaves shade
The trav'lers who
Traverse the glade.

How often do
I travel down
That self-same road
And while I frown
At traffic flow,
Neglect to see
The beauty of
A single tree.

And notice, too,
You're often led
To focus on
What's just ahead.
Instead enjoy
The longer view

Well down the road.
It can seem new.

Imagine when
At your front door
You use your key
To do the chore
Of getting in,
You choose to look
At your front room
As... "Picture Book"!

You'll find things to
Appreciate
About the way
You decorate.
The item you
Say you despise
May look quite nice
With Stranger's Eyes.

The lover of
Those days or years
May have you bored
Almost to tears.
Just try to think
What it was like
When first you two
Came down the pike.

Remember when
You touched her skin?
"Electric" shocks

Came from within!
Remember when
You kissed his lips
Or first enjoyed
His narrow hips?

Remember True
Love's sweet replies
To questions phrased
In your love's eyes?
Remember how
Excited you
Both always felt?
You were not blue.

You might believe
These things are lost
And rediscovery
Will cost.
They haven't gone;
They're in disguise.
Just open up
Your Stranger's Eyes.

REFLECTIONS ON "THE" HOLIDAYS

(WHAT WE CAN LEARN FROM YEAR-END CELEBRATIONS)

I love the holidays at the end of the year. And in my opinion, these are THE holidays! Our year-end celebrations give us an opportunity to reflect on many universally significant and worthwhile values.

Now this is not to say that there are no other times of the year when values can be recognized and celebrated. In fact, I am one who believes that every day should be a holiday, a day worth celebrating. But the last four months of the year in America bring us a concentration of traditional observances that are awe-inspiring when recognized for their positive aspects.

Of course, there are some of us who choose to concentrate on the negative aspects of holidays: they're too commercial; there's too much traffic; certain loved ones aren't around anymore; the "crazies" are all over the place; you know...that kind of stuff. A few of us even dwell on origins of certain holidays pointing out their less than honorable births rather than focusing on the significance of holiday purposes as they have evolved over time.

The word "holiday" stems from the term "Holy Day" which in antiquity usually meant a religious observance with (or without) a festival. In more recent times, it has also come to mean a day free of labor, or one set aside for leisure, fun and recreation, or reflection. I think all of these meanings are appropriate!

For me, it all kind of starts in September when Americans observe Labor Day to recognize the value of work. Nothing is ever accomplished without work. Sometimes the work is quite easy; sometimes it's extremely hard; most times it's somewhere in the continuum between the two. At any rate, in one way or another, the work that someone does or has done is responsible for the materials, security, and freedoms we enjoy. I think it's incredibly important to take a holiday to reward ourselves for the opportunity and capacity to work and the fruits that result from doing it.

To me, Halloween is significant for one very important reason: because it allows us to focus on children and bring joy into their lives. The poorest of kids can don a mask or costume and show up on many doorsteps on the eve of the 31st of October and be showered with treats galore just because they're kids (and it has nothing to do with whose kids they are). And if we are as prudent as we are careful about what we distribute, they may get a little nutrition as well!

November brings the tradition of Thanksgiving and the importance of this holiday is all in the name. Most of us have many, many things for which to be thankful; and in the words of the late, great, gospel icon James Cleveland, "Thank you makes room for more!" The importance of developing an attitude of gratitude is incalculable. And when we can bless the less fortunate out of our plenty, the joy is compounded by our chance to give others something to be thankful for.

In December, the holiday season reaches its apex with celebrations for Christmas, Hanukkah, Kwanzaa and more. The core of all of these traditions is giving. There may be different origins for the giving aspects of these holidays, but no other ones are more significant—especially when we remember that we give of ourselves when we truly give and that it is truly more blessed to give than to receive.

Also in the year's twelfth month, the very last day is often used for reflecting on what has been significant during the preceding 364 1/4 days. It is also for looking forward to making improvements in our lives over the next 364 and a quarter days. New Year's Eve gives us a chance to reflect on what we value, to determine ways to reaffirm the values that work, and to resolve to change the ones that don't.

If we do nothing more in the last four months of each year than recognize the value of work, the value of children, the value of the spirit of thankfulness, and the value of giving, we have done enormous good for ourselves and others. Everything else is icing on the cake…and there's lots of icing!

THANKSGIVING 365

(364 OPPORTUNITIES BEYOND THE NATIONAL HOLIDAY)

Why should we have a Thanksgiving Day? Or maybe we should ask, why do we have <u>only one</u>?

In this country, you don't have to look far to find people who regularly go hungry. And for many who don't have to go hungry, they might not be much better off than those who do. You see, there are those who can't think much about low-fat, no-fat, cholesterol-free, and vitamin enriched food items because the food they can afford is at the bottom of the consumer totem pole. That's why they can afford it.

It's not difficult to find people who have no car, and no home other than the streets. It's easy to find those who have barely enough money to <u>occasionally</u> shop at thrift stores, or make use of public transportation, or visit the local Laundromat.

There are thousands of children in America who have no decent coat to wear to school in the winter and only one decent pair of shoes—if that—for the whole year. Many of these same kids live in homes where there may be little more than cardboard or a sheet of battered plywood to protect against the onslaught of a brisk Arctic wind.

Right here in the United States you can find families lucky enough to have a home but they have no television, no radio, no stereo, no refrigerator, no washer or dryer, no microwave, possibly no stove, and definitely no computer. In these same United States, there are those who have no telephone, no electricity or gas utilities, no running water, and no indoor plumbing.

They may also have a roof that leaks rain, walls that leak air, and floors that offer a view of the ground below. And that's only if they have a floor. There are homes in this nation where the floor and the ground are the same.

There are a great many people in this country who have no health insurance, no life insurance, no car insurance, no Medicare, no Medicaid, and no cash for dentistry, pre-natal care, emergency medical treatment, or routine trips to the doctor or pharmacist.

And yet in this same country, you have people who don't really know what it means to be hungry and to be clueless about how the next food will come. They cannot conceive of what it means to be cold with no hope for warmth except perhaps shared body heat and the chance that you can find or gather enough assorted fabric items to insulate against the cold.

There are people who can't imagine having to walk farther than from the front door to the car and back. There are those who only shop at thrift stores for fun, or only go to a coin-op laundry when the washer at home is broken.

Many folks have more clothes and shoes than they can wear, and enough appliances, electronic gear, and other conveniences to supply another family with one of each without depriving themselves. They enjoy a living environment that is tightly sequestered against the ravages of weather, and the realities of an unprivileged world far different than the one in which they have the freedom to live.

There are those who have access to all that doctors and hospitals have to offer with little or no concern for how to pay for it. These same folks often have more health maintenance latched inside their medicine cabinets than others can acquire if they beg, borrow or steal.

In spite of this great discrepancy between the "Haves" and the "Have-nots," there are those among the "Haves" who don't realize how privileged they are or how easy it is to lose their advantages. And worst of all, they have no idea how to be thankful.

A "Thanksgiving Day" is a wonderful observance. But the great sadness for me is that most people think it only comes once a year and that it has everything to do with over-indulgence and nothing to do with giving.

The best thanks giving is whatever we can give with joy from the bounty of our privileges with no need to be recognized or thanked for our gifts. The second-best <u>thanks</u> giving is the <u>thanks</u> we give out of the sheer joy of knowing how blessed we are—even if we have comparatively little to begin with.

In my view, the <u>national holiday</u> called Thanksgiving is a distant third.

GIVING THANKS FOR EVERYTHING

(REMEMBERING TO OBSERVE RATHER THAN JUDGE)

The last time you celebrated Thanksgiving, did you really take time during the week to feel gratitude? And did you remember to give thanks for <u>everything</u>?

Sometimes we forget to be thankful altogether; but it's really hard to do that during the Thanksgiving Holiday when so many of us are feasting and enjoying the company of loved ones. For a personal example, I spent one fairly recent Thanksgiving with my wife's extended family as we celebrated her grandfather's 100th birthday. I think a hundred years for a single human life is a lot to be thankful for—even if it's not my own. It's a tiny drop in the bucket compared to the entire expanse of time; but on a mortal scale, it's enormous. And I suspect the ups and downs over the course of a lifetime like that can be gargantuan. I know they have been significant for me; and I'm still short of a mere half-century milestone of life.

But again, the ups of life are a lot easier to celebrate than the downs. I'm more and more convinced, though, that the downs must be celebrated also. In fact, the downs may not be "downs" at all. Our <u>judgment</u> about the value of an event is not necessarily the same as its true value. So try to be thankful even for your so-called down times. They have gifts for you, too.

Let's not forget that challenges give us opportunities to stretch and exercise the figurative muscles of our human beingness. We are potentially stronger in a variety of ways for every challenge that we meet head on—especially if we work to discern what we can gain from so doing.

When we have aches and pains, let's be sure to take note of all the places where pain <u>could</u> be occurring in our bodies but is <u>not</u>. And whatever pain we feel, let's imagine that it could be twice or three times as bad... and then be thankful that it's not. Let's also be aware that pain is always a message to us about choices—either past ones we need to work to correct, or present ones we need to make for the sake of possibly a more pain free future. And when we can't seem to escape pain in the body or soul, let's work even harder to determine what that means; because we can be certain that it means something.

If we experience loss, there is likely still something we can gain. If we can't seem to get what we want or need, maybe we need to give more of what we <u>do</u> have. If we are afraid, let's remember that fear, itself, is still the only thing we should actually get any where near fearing. If trouble seems to be headed our way, let's assume that it is nothing we can't handle, and be thankful for the opportunity to prove that we can.

Never forget that we can be thankful for sunshine everyday—even when we don't directly see it or feel it. Never forget that things can't get so bad that they couldn't be worse. Never forget that where one person sees bitter chocolate and sour lemons, another can see chocolate mousse and lemon meringue pie. Perspective and leverage work wonders and miracles everyday; but it all depends on where you stand and how you interpret what you see, feel and do from that vantage point.

As the character, Forrest Gump, says, "Life is like a box of chocolates; you never know what you're gonna get." And furthermore, if a worm or two gets to the candy before you do, just remember that science tells us it's just extra protein. Be thankful.

H.A.P.P.Y. N.E.W. Y.E.A.R.
(AN ACROSTIC GREETING)

appy New Year!!! Wouldn't it be nice to share that greeting everyday? Of course, there are only a few official New Year's Days, and barring some serendipitous coincidence, this is probably not one of them. Nevertheless, I'd like to wish you a happy new year. After all, today is the first day of the rest of your next year from today; so it works for me.

Also, whether you formally made resolutions for the last official New Year or not, I hope you are taking advantage of opportunities to renew your life in ways that seem appropriate for you. But if not, there's no better time than the present. In fact, some would say there is no <u>other</u> time than the present...but that's a discussion for <u>another</u> time.

For <u>today</u>, however, let's give "HAPPY NEW YEAR" some additional meaning. Let's use the letters that spell it out to remind ourselves of some things we may want to take along on our respective journeys through the next 365 days.

"**H**" will be for "**health.**" In a world where there are so many agents that can <u>rob</u> us of health, it is definitely a privilege to be healthy; but it comes at a price. The cost is a regular effort to preserve what we have and continually improve it. Let's be sure to make the effort. Our very lives depend on it.

"**A**" will represent "**attentiveness.**" We really need to pay better attention to our experience. There's too much that we miss as we rush through our lives as if getting to the end of it were the goal rather than enjoying the ride. Stop and smell the roses! Wake up and smell the coffee! If something stinks, dispose of it! Pay attention!

"**P**" can be for "**preparedness.**" You don't have to be one of those people who never go anywhere without a Swiss Army knife, an umbrella, and a parachute; but try to be prepared...or at least resourceful. Anticipate your needs as best you can and be prepared to meet *them* as well as the things that you *can't* expect but must deal with nevertheless.

"**P**" can also be for "**perseverance.**" There's no substitute for good old-fashioned "stick-to-it-ivenesss." Old sayings remind us that if things are worth having, they are also worth working for and waiting for. Persevere. Don't give up on what's important.

"**Y**" might be for "**youthfulness.**" A world of youth is a world of freshness and vitality and non-jadedness. It is a world of wonder and surprise and openness. It is a world of innocence and humor and tolerance. It is a world of resilience. It is a world we would do well to be in touch with in every way possible and for as long as possible.

"**N**" is for "**niceties.**" "Random kindness and senseless acts of beauty" are worth propagating incessantly. In every situation, ask yourself what is the most loving thing to do, and then do it. Be nice.

"**E**" stands for enthusiasm. Life is both too short and too wonderful to go through lackadaisically. Be enthusiastic. Let no circumstances rob you of the joy that will always emanate from within if you allow it by cultivating your enthusiasm. Do it now!

"**W**" will represent "**wonder**" in our acrostic. Wonder about things the way you used to before you decided you had it all figured out. Remember to look not only for the answers to your questions but for the questions to your answers. The more we know, the more we understand that we know very little of what can be known. Keep wonder alive.

"**Y**" (as we come to it again) reminds us to be "**yea-sayers**" rather than naysayers. Let's be positive and affirmative. Let's be into "possibility thinking" rather than allowing ourselves the dubious luxury of believing in so much *im*possibility. We have had enough of "Just Say No!" What will we say "yes" to?

"**E**" will stand for "**expeditiousness.**" Being efficient and speedy is definitely to our advantage in a society that increasingly expects us *all* to do *more* with *less*. It may not be fair, but it's the way of the world. Get used to it. Batten down the hatches, tighten up the ship, dodge the torpedoes, and go full speed ahead whenever possible.

"**A**" brings us to **adjustability.**" We are in deep trouble if we can't be flexible. In spite of our best efforts, things will sometimes (if not often) simply not go the way we've planned. Not to worry. Go to plan "C" or plan

"J." As my mom used to always say, "there's more than one way to skin a cat." Be flexible.

"R" (last, but not least) will herald the word **"respectfulness."** How sweet it would be, indeed, if we could all learn to be more respectful of one another, and of nature, and of ourselves. And that's "enough said."

Happy New Year! Perhaps the greeting and the thought will remind you to think of your **health, attentiveness, preparedness, perseverance, youthfulness, niceties, enthusiasm, wonder, yea saying, expeditiousness, adjustability, and respectfulness.**

SELF-AFFIRMATIONS
(WRITING RESOLUTIONS THAT MAKE A DIFFERENCE)

Whether it's the New Year or not, if you want to make resolutions that really have some teeth in them, you could try writing self-affirmations instead of resolutions. Most people don't do that, you know. Resolutions are simply statements that show your determination to do something. Self-affirmations allow you to assertively state something for yourself as already true—even if there is no current evidence that it is. And even though that may sound illogical, it's a process that works like magic.

Resolutions can be easily ignored, denied, forgotten, or discounted. You should know. You probably know someone for whom that has been true in the past...present company excluded, of course. But affirmations, when correctly done can literally reprogram your brain and your experience for success.

I'd like to give you a simple formula for creating self-affirmations that actually works; so if you're interested, grab a pencil and a scrap of paper and you'll be able to get started right away. That's helpful for those of us who like instant gratification.

But before I tell you what the formula is, I want to point out that the principle behind it is not new by any means. A whole field of scientific study called neurolinguistic programming has grown up around the principle in recent years. But Solomon, who is said to be one of the wisest men who ever lived, summed it up quite nicely a couple of thousand years ago when he wrote, "As a Man thinketh in his heart, so is he...."

Now if Solomon had been writing today, he no doubt would have written, "As a man or woman thinketh in his or her heart so is he or she." After all, he was bound to be smart enough to be politically correct. Nevertheless, the truth of what he wrote is unassailable...so much so, that it has been repeated a few times in other ways, by other folks.

Both Henry Ford and Mark Twain are quoted as saying, "If you think you can or if you think you can't, you're right!" Henry was born nearly thirty years after Mark, so we'll give the latter the benefit of originality. But the wisdom is the same as Solomon's.

In Richard Bach's book <u>Illusions...</u>, he writes, "Argue for your limitations, and sure enough they're yours." Different words; flip side of the coin; but the same idea. And then you will also remember that <u>"The Little Engine That Could"</u> did because it started off by saying, "I think I can!" (And by the way, let's not forget that there was a great deal of enthusiasm invested in that affirmation, also.)

Okay...if you have your pencil ready, I want you to write four terms down in list form, saving a little room for definitions in between just in case. Here we go:

I...
NOW...
EXACTLY WHAT...
WHEN....

That's it. Now, let's look at what it means.

The "I" represents first person singular pronouns. When you write your self-affirmations, make sure they say "I," "me," and "myself," but no "yous," no "its" and no "theys." In this case, you don't need someone or something else to affirm you.

Try also to write or speak your affirmation without using the word "not." Positive statements are more easily assimilated by the concrete processor of the brain than abstract, negative ones.

"NOW" is an adverb that represents a present tense verb. If you start with "I," you might want to write I *am*, I *can*, I *feel*, I *do*, I *see*, I *know*, I *believe*, I *understand*...That's all <u>now</u> as opposed to I <u>will</u> or I *had* or I *did*, which is <u>not</u> now. As with affirmative versus negative language, your brain functions better in the concrete present than in the abstract future or past.

The "EXACTLY WHAT" phrase means (more or less) exactly that. It's what you want to affirm in terms that are as exact as you can state them.

The more exact you are, the better. The brain doesn't embrace fuzzy, vague ideas as well as it does sharp and clear ones.

"WHEN" means a reasonable deadline. If you don't give yourself a reasonable deadline, you either give yourself forever (in which case, you'll take forever) or you try to do too much more quickly than is reasonable. Both are deadly.

Now...a quick example before we move on. For the sake of illustration, let's say you want to lose five pounds after the holidays (Good choice, huh!) and your target weight is 120 pounds. You might write: "I feel wonderful weighing 120 good-looking, powerful, healthy, and sexy pounds by February 15, 1995." If you check, you'll see that every element of the formula is included. "I" (first person singular pronoun) "feel" (present tense verb) "wonderful weighing 120 good-looking, powerful, healthy, and sexy pounds" (the exactly what) "by February 15, 1995," (the reasonable deadline.)

Of course, your numbers and your words would probably be different; but as long as you cover the basics, write the affirmation, copy it, and place it in strategic locations where you can't help but see it regularly, you'll be way ahead of the game. And then, if you recite it or meditate on it with enthusiasm every time you see it, the message will soon be internalized as a truth. When that happens, you're almost home free. You cannot be different than what you firmly believe you are.

Now you may think this is too simple to be effective; but if you got it, you can get it to happen for you. I guarantee it.

REAFFIRMING RELATIONSHIPS

Sometime in December (or a little earlier if we're really efficient), in my household, we send out holiday greeting cards and Christmas letters to many of our friends and family members. Some of these folks we don't get to see, touch or talk to all year long. That's one of the reasons why we prioritize it every year even though it turns into a major project and does come at some expense for cards or letters, postage, and printing. We care about the people we love and we say to ourselves, "Even if this is the only time all year that we are in touch, we'll be sure that this contact with our loved one is meaningful." We feel like it's the least we can do to make up for the fact that daily living often precludes the kind of contact we would like to have.

Actually, I can't think of a better time to reach out and touch people. This is the time of year when most of us seek opportunities to connect with other people who bring joy to our lives. It's also the time of year when some of us start thinking about those annual "New Year's Resolutions." It's as good a time as any to strengthen our connections with people who are special to us.

We don't have to wait for a holiday motivation, though. At any time we choose, we can take advantage of ways to reaffirm our commitment to relationships. We have husbands, and wives, and boyfriends, and girlfriends, and children, and grandchildren, and siblings, and parents, and grandparents, and cousins, and nieces, and nephews, and even great-relatives more than two generations removed from us. On top of that there are usually hosts of friends, acquaintances, associates, co-workers, clients, servers, and even relative strangers that impact our lives in significant ways. Are we as committed to these relationships as we <u>can</u> be? Are we as committed to these relationships as we would <u>like</u> to be? Are we as committed to these relationships as we <u>should</u> be? Is our commitment reflected in what we do, what we say, what we think, and what we feel?

We are the ones who are best qualified to answer these questions for ourselves. In fact, no one else IS qualified—not even the people with whom we have relationships. They will certainly have their <u>perspectives</u> on our level of commitment to them; but even if they <u>have</u> an opinion about whether we're as committed as we can be or should be, only we can know for sure. And even if they are able to relate to how our commitment is reflected in our actions, only we can know how it relates to our thoughts and feelings and motivations.

One thing is certain, we cannot keep relationships alive without feeding them regularly; and making them <u>thrive</u> is (in the same way) practically out of the question. And though it is a well-worn cliché, we must also know that relationships are a two-way street: people who are in them must <u>give</u>... <u>and</u> <u>receive</u> to keep them thriving. And what better time to talk about giving and receiving than now.

No matter what season it is, let's give and receive more love, more kindness, more caring, more consideration, more help, more offerings of peace, more leeway, more beauty, more of ourselves. And let's be certain to give more and more thought to how we can continually improve all the relationships we have. It is an often unspoken but never unbroken "Law of the Universe" that what we give of ourselves comes back to us. We must continue to learn how this law manifests in our lives, because it is certain that it does. If we want to <u>receive</u> more <u>from</u> our relationships we must <u>give</u> more <u>to</u> them. Please...let's do that.

DISTANT REPLAY
(BRINGING THE BEST FROM THE PAST TO THE FUTURE)

On the television network, ESPN, there is a special feature called "Distant Replay." Obviously, it is a wordplay take-off on the ubiquitous "Instant Replay" phenomenon born of videotape technology where an interesting occurrence in a current sports event is immediately replayed for the viewer's enjoyment or discovery. The "Distant Replay," however, as you either know (or might suspect) replays some noteworthy event from a past sports event.

It occurs to me that an appropriate time for each of us to replay some of the better events from our past is "New Year's Day." The first of the year heralds a traditional, annual new beginning for many of us. But whether you observe the New Year on January 1st or at some other time of the year doesn't matter nearly as much as what you do with the auspicious occasion.

There's something decidedly refreshing about an official new year. For anyone who chooses, it is an opportunity to reflect on the close of the current year while making plans for the ensuing one. It is a chance to renew commitments and make resolutions and plans. It is a time for change, or for deciding to continue the good things that have brought you successfully to the moment. And it may be a moment that we would do well to fill with a few of our favorite "Distant Replays."

I'm not one who recommends that we dwell on the past or attempt to relive it. I think that's folly. There's probably nothing sadder than the former high school quarterback who keeps reliving the touchdown pass he threw to win the state championship twenty years before and forcing others to relive it with him. And wouldn't we like to forget the prom queen who never grew past the popularity-seeking mentality that got her the crown but kept her from developing her mind to a level that would help her realize her greater potentials.

On the other hand, I strongly advocate for remembering the high moments of the past and remembering the qualities that helped you achieve those moments. It is those qualities that may help you realize continuing successes. If there were memorable episodes in your past of courage, or caring, or good fortune, or learning, or teaching, or surprise, or beauty, or floods of emotion, you might do very well indeed to remember what got you there; for these are the things that may carry you ever forward.

In one of my "Distant Replays", I remember being encouraged to deliver a commencement address for graduating seniors at my college alma mater while I was still an undergrad. Taking that challenge taught me things about myself as a writer and public speaker that I might never have learned if someone had not seen that potential in me and nudged me along.

In another, I remember the joy of witnessing my son's birth after a doctor's empirical prognosis had me believing I would probably never have children of my own.

You may call it whatever you like, but I call it a blessing. It gave me an intensely personal experience with the reality of miracles. I expect more of them.

Another memory comes back of having undertaken a trip by car as a young man with what I thought was just enough money to get me where I needed to go. With the gas gage registering nearly empty and my destination still miles away, I drove to the nearest church to ask a 24-hour loan from what I hoped would be an available kind pastor. Instead, my knock went unanswered at the church but a kind parishioner just across the street inquired about my purpose and rescued my trip. Will wonders never cease?

I remember the courage to walk away from a fight when I might just as easily have engaged in heated battle. I remember laughing until tears fell at an irreverent cartoon I saw once. I remember catching a long touchdown pass as a wide receiver in intramural football in college only to have the opposing team insist I was out of bounds. Their judgment stood, but my judgment brings a memory of a reality they can't take away. The touchdown was good!

I remember <u>lots</u> of things, and I remember many of the things that got me to those moments. With the "new year" that begins with each new day, I'm counting on those "Distant Replays" to make my future as rewarding as my past.

ON BLACK HISTORY MONTH
(MUCH OBLIGED TO SPEAK OUT)

Every year—not long after New Year's Day, my mind and heart are assailed by the same distressing conundrum: I have to determine how I will respond to the fact that February is designated as "Black History Month" in America. I always have very mixed feelings.

On the one hand, I am thrilled that for at least one month out of the year, people are encouraged to remember that African-Americans and their descendants have always contributed mightily to the development and success of this nation. On the other hand, I'm bothered that there is not a month for Jewish-American History, and Arab-American History and one each for Latino-Americans, Asian-Americans, and Native Americans—not to mention months for all the other Americans whose ancestry is traced differently than these.

Meanwhile, I'm very thankful to have <u>this</u> space (and others) from which to speak to our <u>common</u> humanity on a regular basis. This is one of the ways that I am a small part of the on-going historical contributions of one of America's many sub-cultures. I embody a portion of the contributions of African-Americans because I <u>am</u> one. Nevertheless, (though there is nothing except my own inner wrestling that says I have to) I dislike feeling somewhat obliged to comment on Black History Month when February rolls around. In fact, on some occasions, I have refused to do so. Like the governmental policies of affirmative action, I think such observances cheapen the contributions of Americans of African (or any) descent at the same time that they provide opportunities that might not otherwise exist.

So the question for me is always: "What should we do with this observance called 'Black History Month'?" If we ignore it, we do so at the peril of ignoring the contributions that made the custom seem like a promising idea in the first place. If we embrace it for four weeks and then conveniently forget about it the rest of the year, what good have we really done? And if we are encouraged to recognize and celebrate Black History, why not Red, Yellow, Brown and White Histories too?

And speaking of "White History," there are those who would say that there is no need to focus on White History (or perhaps more accurately, European-American History) because a huge preponderance of published accounts of history are not only dominated by this particular ethnicity, but by primarily the male half of this cultural equation with barely a nod to the female persuasion. That's why we also have "Women's History Month." And need I say that I feel the same way about this observance that I do about the one I have focused on so far?

Perhaps because February comes in the wake of observances of the Martin Luther King Holiday, it would make sense to allow his prodigious voice to speak on this matter. The dream he articulated in his famous speech tells us very clearly what we must really pursue beyond the tokenism. He didn't necessarily envision periodic observances of the significant historical accomplishments of ignored, unknown or forgotten Americans. Rather, he looked forward to a day when Americans—and all people—"will not be judged by the color of their skin, but by the content of their character."

Perhaps our superficial symbolisms are lesser evils that we must endure until we can pick up American history books and see a balance of information, images and perspectives that reflects the true diversity of America. When we can read any account of history and know that it has been influenced by a whole spectrum of persons of every conceivable description, then I believe we will have arrived at what the interim measures are intended to convey.

A NEW STORY OF CHRISTMAS
(THE "SPIRIT" OF GIVING)

Once Upon A Time, there was a Spirit that came to live among The People. At least, that's what The People thought. For often when they would wonder about certain things, they would suddenly know the answer to what they wondered about. It was almost like magic. They would ask a question and the answer would come in such a powerful flash that they felt as if someone else was present—some unseen person who whispered the answer in their ear. But no one ever saw a soul.

It didn't happen with all of their questions. It seemed to work best when it was a question about needs or the deepest of hearts' desires. And it almost always seemed to work even better when the questions were about someone else rather than about oneself.

It happened to The Baker one day. At least once a week, The Cobbler would come in for bread. Most times he rushed in with a pleasant hello, bought two loaves, and left hurriedly to return to his shop. But at other times he would enter with a furrowed brow, search very carefully for the largest loaf he could find. He would then take a deep breath before he paid for it, sigh again after the money was paid, and walk slowly out of the bakery, with his head down, never saying a word.

The Baker didn't pay much attention at first; but when it started to happen a bit more frequently, one day he said to himself, "I wonder why The Cobbler seems so sad whenever he buys only one loaf of bread." Just as quickly, the answer came to mind, "It's because that is a time when he must choose bread for his family or leather for his shop."

The Baker didn't know why that thought came to mind, but the next time The Cobbler came in and started to carefully survey the loaves, The

Baker found himself saying, "Since you are my twentieth customer today, kind sir, you are entitled to two loaves of bread free. Thank you for being such a good customer!"

The Cobbler smiled broadly and thanked the Baker profusely. It was just the blessing he needed to get ahead with his struggling shoe business. Because of The Baker's kindness, he never again had to sacrifice buying leather to make new shoes so that his family could eat.

The Blacksmith wondered aloud one day about The Farmer who always walked two miles into town and back when he had two perfectly good horses. But the moment he wondered, he suddenly felt that it was because The Farmer's horses had no shoes to protect their feet against the rough terrain between his farm and the town.

One day he told The Farmer that he had more horseshoes than he could use in a year and asked if The Farmer could use a couple of sets for his horses. "Indeed, I can!" he said. "But I can't afford them." Well, to make a long story short, The Blacksmith gave The Farmer two sets of horseshoes and rode out to put them on, too!

It was like that everywhere. The Preacher wondered why The Widow kept to herself so much. And when he suddenly understood that she didn't think she was worthy of being considered for a new marriage, he was more than happy to court and marry her because he had always greatly admired her kindness, her beauty, and her courage.

The Sheriff wondered why he was always arresting The Barber (who was usually a nice guy) for getting drunk and fighting in the saloon. The answer seemed to be that The Barber had no real friends. The Sheriff took him fishing one Sunday afternoon and they became best friends. For some reason, The Barber never fought in the saloon again after that.

The Seamstress wondered why The Doctor, who was otherwise a man of great taste, often wore clothes that were poorly matched. It occurred to her that the matching clothes might be in need of repair so she offered to do his alterations in return for her rheumatism treatments.

Finally as more and more of these occurrences happened, people started to share their experiences. Finally someone figured out that it started happening when The Gambler came to town. He won often enough; but what was more miraculous was that the person who most needed to win always did when The Gambler was involved in a game of cards or pool or darts.

His name was Nicholas. But the funny thing was that when people figured out that he might have been the start of it all, he disappeared without a trace. No one had any idea where he went. After that, people started calling him The Saint.

Soon, The People started hearing stories from other towns about this strange gambler who was not a gambler at all. And everywhere he went, it seems, people learned to recognize the needs of others that they could help fill and a new spirit of giving was born.

After a long time, there were no more reports of Nicholas The Gambler only reports of increased kindnesses that occurred after his coming. And somehow almost every where, people took to calling him Saint Nicholas although in a lot of places, it sounded more like "Santa Claus."

A TWIST ON CHRISTMAS THEMES
(TAKING, CONFLICT, HATE & DEATH)

When the subject is Christmas, one is expected to hold forth on themes such as celebrating new births, giving gifts, establishing peace and spreading love. Well, I don't plan to do that here. Instead, I want to talk about taking, conflict, hate and death. But if you'll stick with me for a few paragraphs, I think you'll discover that these are worthy topics for talking about Christmas.

My dictionary defines the word "taking" as "the act of a person or thing that takes." Since so many gifts are given for Christmas, shouldn't we spend a little time thinking about how they are taken...how they are received or accepted? There was once a commercial on television, for example, where a family received knitted items from a kindly older lady that we can easily assume is a grandmother. Unfortunately, the garments which she presents as sweaters are very seriously flawed, with missing or too-long sleeves, and even one with an absent neck opening.

We last see Granny smiling before the commercial ends, but you might imagine that she will either wind up with hurt feelings or as a victim of needlessly patronizing attitudes marked by faked gratitude. All things being the same, a better way to <u>take</u> the sweaters might be to sincerely thank her for the effort, but to gently point out the flaws and suggest remedies for them. The spirit with which we take what life brings our way is as important as the spirit in which it is given.

Basically, the point of that commercial, by the way, is to try to minimize the disappointment that sometimes accompanies gift-giving and gift-taking by choosing a gift that has an excellent chance of being appreciated by most people. But here is where we can remember that conflict is not necessarily such a bad thing. If what we expect or anticipate doesn't match up with what we receive, for example, maybe that will help us to learn to be less expectant. We might even experience the miracle of learning to be more appreciative of not only what we are given, but what we already possess. That would be a very special miracle, indeed, in a season sometimes marked by excesses of materialism.

Let's remember, too, that almost nothing lasts forever; but even things that do are often merely a shadow of their former selves (like the Parthenon) or stuff we don't really want around (like nuclear waste.) So, expect some of those toys to break, some of those mechanical or electronic items to stop working, and other goods to be lost forever. Most things that are born eventually die—including gifts that are born into new ownership on Christmas day and other days during the season.

Finally, there is at least one thing that you can choose to hate on Christmas…in the sense that hate means "to dislike intensely or passionately." I encourage you to hate the fact that while many of us are inundated with various gifts at this time of the year, there are so many others who <u>expect</u> nothing, who <u>get</u> nothing, and who <u>give</u> nothing, because they <u>have</u> nothing, and those who love them have nothing either. And these people could be us if it were not for certain serendipitous circumstances.

My family hates to see people with nothing. That's why we step up our giving to the have-nots a few more notches during this season. Please join us as we respond to this particular inner <u>hate</u>, <u>take</u> gifts more consciously, de-emphasize the inevitable <u>conflict</u> caused by differences, and celebrate all the precious gifts of life because we know that <u>deaths</u> are inevitable.

LOVE COMES FIRST

Love comes first.
Before we ever hear the word,
Before we feel our hearts are stirred,
Before we find out who we are,
Before we all give in to war,
Before we go out on "A Date",
Before we lead ourselves to hate,
Before we set out on our day,
Before we even kneel to pray,
Love comes first.

Love...comes...first.
When we have found
that patience ends,
When we are critical of friends,
When something angers us inside,
When one considers suicide,
When we create a lovely thing,
When someone moves
our hearts to sing,
When we don't know why we are here,
When we are limited by fear,
Love...comes...first.

Love comes first!
Before we ever come to be,
Before we set all captives free,
Before we give up in despair,
Before we lay emotions bare,
Before we give ourselves away,
Before we find the words to say,
Before we sell our souls for trash,
Before we're blinded by "The Flash",
Love comes first!

Love...comes...first!
Whenever "SEX" is on our minds,
When Holy Matrimony binds,
When any family has pain,
When power's wielded well for gain,
When understanding's needed most,
When someone feels inclined to boast,
When we refuse to reach our heights,
When we skip compromise for fights,
Love...comes...first!

LOVE COMES FIRST!!!
In every single thing we do!
In every thing we're thinking, too!
For every day we're blessed to live!
For every way we choose to give!
To every living creature's heart!
To give our love is how we start!
LOVE COMES FIRST!!!

GIVE YOURSELF A VALENTINE
(ANOTHER POSITIVE SELF-AFFIRMATION)

The next time you go out to get Valentines for loved ones, I have a suggestion for you: give a Valentine to yourself.

I'm serious. After you've browsed through rack after rack of greetings, scouring the displays for that perfect card for your wife, your boyfriend, your nephew, your boss or your granny, take a few minutes to find the perfect card for you. Better yet, make your own Valentine's Day greeting card the first one you buy. And if you've got the time, the inclination and some basic materials, I have an even more awesome idea: make the card instead of buying it!

Think about it for a minute. How do you feel when you receive a Valentine's Day sentiment from someone who obviously invested a lot in its selection or creation? How do you feel when you get a Valentine that's tailored just for you? It's really nice, isn't it? Well why wait for someone else to make the investment? Give yourself the card you'd love to get from someone else! And don't pick one of those generic "one-size-fits-all" cards either.

You see, in this case, it's really the path of least investment to choose a card that has a greeting like this:

> "On Valentine's, the perfect day to touch the one you love, I want you to be sure to know it's you I'm thinking of!"

Gosh, all you need after that is to sign it "Sincerely, Yours Truly" and you've got it made. Yeccchh!!!

Now I don't mean to disparage simplicity. In fact, a card like that might be perfect coming from a kindergartner or someone who's tentative about making a declaration of love. But to express love to someone that's really special, a reasonably intelligent, thoughtful and creative person like you can do much better—especially since there are talented folks who design and market great greeting cards. And what better person for you to show how much you care than yourself?

So, browse through the displays of Hallmark, and Ambassador, and Blue Mountain, and others...with <u>yourself</u> in mind. Find an affirmation of love for yourself that you can proudly display on your desk or bulletin board or dresser. Then, from time to time, read it and remember that on the day you chose or created it, you regarded yourself with the kind of love expressed by the card. Perhaps you'll realize that you deserve that kind of love from you everyday.

But don't forget, if you can't <u>find</u> the perfect card, you can make one. It doesn't have to be flawless, just the best you can do at the time you create it. That way, you can be sure to say exactly what you want to say to affirm yourself. Maybe you can make a card that says something like:

> **In all the world,**
> **no one like you has ever crossed my trail.**
> **You stand by me**
> **through thick and thin when other comrades fail.**
> **I choose, this day,**
> **to let you know what you have meant to me,**
> **And trust that you**
> **will always know you'll have true love from me.**

Okay, maybe that's a little hokey for you. If it is, go for a bit of humor. Find a little mirror somewhere and glue it on the front of a folded card above the words:

> **"If you could earn a million dollars for loving**
> **the person you see on the front of this card,**
> **would you do it?"**

Then on the inside, it could say,

**"If you answered yes,
that's worth more than a million dollars!
If you said no,
no wonder you're broke!"**

I thought about sharing with you the message on <u>my</u> card to myself; but hey, it's a little personal. If you <u>really</u> want to know what it says, you'll have to ask.

INTIMATE FRIENDS
(BEGINNING TO SEE THE NEED)

I think a lot about my best friends. Actually, I like to celebrate them. I have some very beautiful best friends; and they bring joys to my life that are practically incalculable. My best words fall far short of really describing what they mean in my life.

There's something you need to understand, though. I have lots of friends. People who show themselves friendly often do; and I have done that for a long time. I had some of the world's greatest role models for friendliness in my parents. They got me off to a wonderful start. But I 'm not talking about celebrating all of my friends at the moment. I'm talking about the best friends, my intimate friends.

I'm not even talking about my good friends. I have some really good friends; people that I love to be with (and who love to be with me); people that I enjoy; people that I can count on; people who matter to me in a really big way. But there is another set of friends even greater than these. These are the best friends. These are my intimate friends. These are the friends that I couldn't trade for anything—not even for all of my other friends put together.

For me, the very best of my special friends is my wife. I can't begin to tell you in this time and space all the reasons why she is my best friend of all; but I can tell you that she is irreplaceable in my life. She is the person who is the one element of support for me that outranks every other source of support except for what comes from my spiritual beliefs. When you have a friend that means that much to you, every other reason why that person is your friend seems like a minor detail by comparison. And if that person is your mate for life, you have scored a major coup.

If more of us would choose a mate who is also our best friend, our society would be marred by far fewer divorces and so-called "broken homes." But too often we mate for reasons that are more like skim milk than whole, more like a go cart than an automobile, more like a pup tent than a mansion, more for selfishness than sel<u>fless</u>ness.

Of course, circumstances may <u>prevent</u> us from marrying our very <u>best</u> friends. If my wife's name were Dennis rather than Denise, for example, that would present quite a matrimonial problem for me. But what it would <u>not</u> do is prevent me from having her (or him as the case might be) as an intimate friend.

Unfortunately, most of us still hold on to the romantic fantasy of being able to find a single person in our lives that can provide for every need we have from a relationship with another human being. Most of us will never have that. One reason is because the persons who could be the perfect complements for us are very hard to find. Another is that most of us are not persistent, patient and faithful enough to look for them and find them.

What we need, I think is to learn to develop intimate friendships. We need to discover those people with whom we can share an unconditional love. We need to find people who light up like Christmas trees when ever we are near and who cause us to glow likewise. We should long for people in our lives that are like a breath of fresh air whenever we are in their presence.

There ought to be a person in our lives that can hold us in an embrace in a way that creates a cocoon of love that allows us to feel safe and warm. There ought to be a person who can kiss us and make the world stand still. There ought to be people who can make us tingle all over with just a glance, or a smile, or the sound of their voices, or a combination of words jotted on a thank you card presented to us for doing something for which we expected no special thanks.

There ought to be a person in our lives who shares gifts with us just because we are loved. There ought to be a person with whom we feel totally connected even though we may be miles apart. There ought to be a person who picks up the phone to call at almost precisely the moment we are thinking thoughts of love about him or her. There ought to be a person who causes as much excitement for us as being on our favorite ride at an amusement park.

It would be nice if the person who could do all that for us was one and the same, but in real life, it is not likely. But with the right group of intimate friends who love us unconditionally, anything and everything is possible.

A HEART SO BIG
(UNDERSTANDING OUR CAPACITY TO LOVE AND CARE)

Have you ever not been able to love someone that you wanted to love because you didn't have the capacity to do it? I doubt it. When you think about it, it has probably never happened for you or anyone.

Let's do think about it. Some parents choose to have large families. My mother, for example, grew up in a family of thirteen siblings, and my grandpa had been married before and had fathered another half dozen or so with that wife. Do you think he ever said to my grandmother, "Susan, we better not have any more kids. I've plumb run out of enough love in my heart to go around?" I don't think so.

Think about the relatives you have that you love. There may be any number of siblings, parents, children, cousins, aunts, uncles, nieces and nephews that get a healthy piece of your heart. Although they may not all get healthy pieces of your life, they are all loved. No one has to do without when someone gets an extra helping of love. Am I not right?

Now, think about your friends…I mean your good friends…the ones that you dearly love. You may have only a few, or you may literally have tons of them. But I'd be willing to bet that no matter how many of them you have, you never have to rob Peter to love Paul (so to speak) and you never run out of room.

When it comes to love, we have big, cavernous hearts. There is no limit to our capacity to love. If you've ever thought there was a limit, think again. What is limited is our ability to express the love we know and feel; and even that is limited less than we might think.

There are boundaries that are often a frustration for those who love and those who would be loved. Love is nothing if it is not expressed, or if it is expressed in ways that are not understood or appreciated by the loved one. Sometimes to declare love is to set up an expectation that the declaration will be followed by other suitable expressions. Unfortunately, that is not always possible, proper or mutually desired.

Let's face it; although feeling love may be natural, effortless, and limitless, the expression of what we feel takes time, energy and effort—not to mention creativity, courage, communication, motivation, willingness, and permission to name a few others. That's where the boundary lines lie for most of us—not in the capacity to love.

Sometimes the declaration itself is enough...and sometimes it's not. This is among the many reasons that communication is a key to handling the explosive power of love. Courage is always required because sharing love breeds relationships and relationships bring challenges. Creativity is necessary because no two people have the exact same language of love. We have to learn to speak love to one another in languages we each understand.

Time, energy, effort, motivation, willingness, permission...a case can be made for all of these and more as to their necessity for the expression of love. But practically nothing is required for us to learn to feel love for another...except a good model or two. When we are loved, we learn to love.

If everyone who had the capacity to love expressed their love appropriately and as fully as possible; and if everyone who had the need for love to be shared would simply ask for what they needed until they found someone who had it to share, what do you suppose would happen? Would there be anyone who would have to go without?

Is it possible that hatred could exist at all in a world where everyone was loving and being loved as much as possible or needed? I don't believe it could; but if we're careless, hatred, alone, can eventually overwhelm and destroy us.

I believe we have to be assertive about asking for the love we need and about sharing the love we have. I often ask for permission to hug people. I am almost never refused. And a funny thing happens when you give someone a hug: you often get one, too—even if your motivation for giving one is completely unselfish!

I sometimes see people I think could use a hug but don't volunteer for the duty. Maybe I just don't feel invited. But that's probably an adult hang-up. I've also seen big, powerful, stone-faced men melt in the spontaneous warmth of a hug from a loving four-year old too innocent to be hung-up.

If only we could all love that way!

MULTILINGUAL LOVE
(DISCOVERING THE LANGUAGES OF LOVE THAT WE SPEAK)

What is your language of love? We all have different ones, you know. We learn to speak love in much the same way we learn to speak English, or Spanish, or Russian, or Lakota, or Chinese. We interact with people who speak a certain language of love and we basically adopt their expressions, inflections, and meanings. Eventually, we color them with our own experiences, personalities and intentions.

So what is your language of love? Where and from whom have you learned it? How was it (and is it) spoken by the people with whom you interact? How is it expressed and with what inflections or intensity? What are the meanings of love in your life and how has your command of the languages of love been colored, influenced, limited, or expanded by your experience, personality or intentions? And last, but not least, are you multilingual?

This last question is more important than you might think. The subtleties inherent in how we each choose to express our love for one another are mind-boggling. Unless we have a multilingual approach to expressing love, we'll miss many opportunities to share the best of ourselves and our love with each other.

Even if we speak more or less the same love language, the nuances can be as unsettling as the English language can be when it is spoken as a first language by Brits, Americans, Scots, Irish or Welshmen or as a second language by Germans, Hispanics, Southeast Asians, Russians, or the Chinese. If you think English is the same no matter who speaks it, you have led a very sheltered life!

In the same way, for example, we may grow up in families where hugs are part of the language of love. And yet the quality of those hugs can range from brief and perfunctory, sideways squeezes done primarily out of a sense of duty (and perhaps inconvenience) to long, lingering, frontal and full-bodied love attacks imbued with highly emotional and even sensual overtones. We definitely do not all have the same experience of hugging in our families of origin.

And yet, the family situations in which we come into our own as human beings are the primary source of the languages we learn. This is true whether we consider our mother tongue, our body language, or our language of love.

As with verbal speech, we use our language of love as we expect to have others use that language with us. We take it for granted when we speak that we will be understood and that when others speak, we will understand them. It's only when we get a "No comprendo!" that we realize there may be a problem.

Even more frightening, though, is that we speak our love languages of choice and are responded to in ways that make us feel as if we are really communicating; and then we discover later that we were completely misunderstood. That is a supremely frustrating occurrence when it involves languages of love.

When you speak your language of love, how do you know when it is being understood? How do you know when it's not? How do you find out what language someone else speaks? Do you ask them? How do you make your vernacular of love known? Do you tell? What happens when the languages of loved ones don't match, and what does one do about it? How important is it to be a multilingual dialectician when it comes to speaking love?

I believe these are incredibly important questions. If my language of love has to do with giving and receiving high touch (like kisses and hugs and strokes and snuggles and massages) what happens when yours is different? What happens when your preferred modes of expressing love have to do with gifts, and shared experiences, and tender words and love letters, and doing things for loved ones but touch is something you come to as an afterthought—if at all? When it comes to love's vernacular, I think we are in trouble unless we are at least bilingual!

We expect to be loved the way we do love; but that's a dangerous expectation. We have to know when our language of love is being understood and when it is not. We have to discover ways to find out what language someone else speaks and help them to find out what our expression of love is.

Whether we ask or tell, we have to do all we can to ensure that how we express love with one another matches as much as possible. Being multilingual lovers increases our chances of speaking love in ways that all our loved ones can appreciate. And what good is expressing love if it cannot be received in the same spirit with which it is given?

If you don't know the subtle or at least the blatant differences between you and your loved ones when it comes to "lovespeak," I cannot suggest more strongly that you hurry to an understanding as soon as possible.

UNCONDITIONAL LOVE
(BEYOND ROMANCE, SEX & MARITAL BLISS)

Shall we talk about love again? Oh, why not?! There's certainly enough discussion about other things that are a lot less interesting or important. So we might as well take a chance that a few moments together will encourage us to at least think about love. Don't you think so? Well, anyway, here's another thought or two.

First of all, we must never forget that love comes in a multitude of gradations sort of like intensities of light. It ranges from the level of a single small candle to unimaginable, blinding brilliance; from just a little bit more than "like" to the ultimate in unconditional love. Of course, most of us can't conceive of being able to reach the ultimate. In fact, most of us don't believe we'll even get close. A lot of that has to do with all the things with which we confuse love.

We confuse love with peace, infatuation, romance, sex, contentment, sensitivity, perfection, communication, happiness, marriage…and a boomerang. All of these things may be related (like in a family) but they are not the same. And some of them are only about as related as you would be to the husband of the second cousin of the woman that's married to your wife's brother. You've got to stretch a little to get the two of you in the same family!

Love is not peace. If a person loves him- or herself, that can create inner peace—but only if the love is unconditional. (More about that later.)

If a person loves another, and is loved by that person, they may, indeed, have a peaceful relationship; but it is still best when the love is unconditional. And if agape (spontaneous, altruistic) love were universal and reciprocal, it could create peace in the world. But it's not, and unless it is, it can't.

The terms love and peace are definitely not synonymous and are related only with effort.

Love is not infatuation, romance, sex, or marriage! Infatuation is marked by the foolishness of loving that which is either unknown to you or which you imbue with qualities that the beloved may or may not possess. Romance is usually characterized by a sense of adventure and mystery, continuous discovery, and the willingness or tendency to minimize faults while basking happily in the illusion created by focusing on virtues.

Romance is the home of the expression "in love" which is seldom if ever seriously used where romance does not exist; but romance can exist with or without love. So can erotic passion. And so can marriage.

Love is not contentment, happiness, sensitivity, perfection, or communication; and it's definitely not a boomerang.

We often expect that when we love someone and that someone loves us, we will be happy and content. We also usually anticipate that the other will be sensitive to our needs, eventually match all of our expectations, and practically know what we're thinking without our saying it thus making communication easy if not redundant.

And above all, it seems, we believe that every expression of love we direct in some way to our beloved will be reflected back to us immediately by that person with the same intent and intensity just as if it were some sort of love boomerang.

Now, mind you, it could happen, and it sometimes does. But we are smart not to expect it.

In certain relationships, it is all right to want peace, romance, passion, contentment, sensitivity, a degree of perfection, excellent communication, happiness, commitment, and reciprocity. It's just not all right to assume that these things are a natural outgrowth of love—even if it is unconditional love... especially if it is unconditional love.

And what is unconditional love?

When love is unconditional, it is given freely, openly, and without expectation. It is unselfish, undemanding, spontaneous and other-centered. It has integrity whether it is reciprocated or not. Although it may be related to any of the following, it is nevertheless separate from generic happiness, separate from marital happiness, separate from carnal gratification, and separate from whether you like someone or not, or at some particular time may be unhappy with someone. It is not romance and it is not in any way deterred by hatred or any other emotion from within or without.

When one loves unconditionally, one says, "I love you." Period. It is not "I love you if" or "I love you because" or "I love you when." To love unconditionally means that love never dies—even when there is little or no peace, romance, passion, contentment, sensitivity, communication, happiness, or commitment…and/or no boomerang.

To love unconditionally is difficult; but it is possible. And it may even be necessary. However, none of us are likely to live long enough to see unconditional love become a universal reality. Nevertheless, in the meantime, we will unfortunately see too much of what occurs because of our failure to <u>make</u> it ubiquitous.

Too bad.

THE NECESSITY OF UNCONDITIONAL LOVE
(WHY UNCONDITIONAL LOVE MATTERS MOST)

Sometimes the people who need love the most are the ones who get it the least. That is doubly unfortunate because often the people who receive love the least are the ones who are least likely to have the capacity for loving others.

Love is learned. So is hatred. Caring is learned. So is indifference. Tolerance is learned. So is prejudice. Kindness is learned. So is violence.

The poem entitled *"Children Learn What They Live"* is a poignant elaboration on the meaning that is encapsulated quite nicely in the title. Children learn what they live. People learn what they live.

We are exposed to the idea that love is conditional through the environments in which we learn to be human. If for no other reason than that, we should learn to love with as few conditions as possible. What is really true about love is not necessarily the same as what we learn from being socialized in our environments.

Obviously, the best place to create that environment of love is in the home. But assuming that many kids won't get the message there, they will have to get it—if they get it at all—somewhere else. That's where you come in.

You see it's really easy to get the conditional message. Kids learn this version of truth even when it is not said in so many words. Behavior communicates messages that are often more powerful than the words we speak.

Kids hear messages like, "I love you when you don't wet your bed;" "I love you when you make good grades;" "I love you because you don't get on my nerves;" "I love you if you don't make my life more unpleasant than it already is;" I love you when it's convenient for me; "I love you when you make me smile;" "I love you because you do something, or say something, or don't do something, or don't say something that I find objectionable."

Unfortunately, children who grow up with these messages become adults who expect communication to continue unfolding in the same way. So they simply deliver adult versions of the same messages and expectations they heard, and then often add others.

Adults say, "I love you because you turn me on;" "I love you because you make me happy;" "I love you when you behave as I expect you to;" "I love you if you are never the source of unpleasant surprises;" "I love you when you ignore your own needs for the sake of mine;" "I love you because you never confront me with my faults;" or "I love you because you love me."

Of course, the implication is that love is withheld or non-existent when the conditions are not met. We find ourselves choosing to alter the persons that we are or the behaviors that seem most natural to us in order to please someone who promises to love us only if we do. We then become angry, frustrated and resentful and often don't know why because we expect mutual love to be a panacea that erases these kinds of difficulties.

The problem is not with love; the problem is that we learn to love with conditions attached. Love should be no more conditional than sunshine. The sun does not refuse to rise and shine because of some behavior that we do or do not exhibit. It rises everyday. There are days when we may not see it from the ground, but it is always there. If we rise up above the fog, or smog, or clouds, or mountains that obscure it, we find it right where it belongs.

If we love someone, our love should be like sunshine—always there regardless of the conditions that arise between us. We may not love certain behaviors; we may not love certain conditions; but we should not necessarily confuse those things with the actual persons in our experience.

There might be times when we don't like the persons we love. There may be times when we don't want to be near them. Occasionally, we may be really angry with them. From time to time, they may disappoint us terribly. But let's not for a moment believe that these feelings are an excuse to withdraw our love. In fact, if we can withdraw our love, it may very well not have been love in the first place.

Real love never dies, and it's often difficult to pinpoint its moment of birth. Once you really love someone, you always do—if it's real love… mature love. That's one way we can account for someone who continues to welcome back a person who has treated them badly. In this case, there is nothing wrong with them loving the person who mistreats them; the problem is that they don't love themselves enough to choose not to live with the pain and suffering that their mate inflicts. Sometimes you have to love people enough to let them go or ask them to leave—even when that someone is you.

You may know or have already guessed that invariably there are a lot of conditions that complicate matters in loving relationships. Suffice it to say for now, then, that for us to love ourselves and to love others unconditionally will teach us all more about what love really is. It will also simplify a great deal of what conditional love has complicated.

THE THREE L'S
(ON LIVING, LOVING AND LEARNING)

I have some observations that stem from an experience that is intensely personal. But at the same time, the concepts I'd like to highlight and their importance to each of us are incredibly universal.

On September 3, 1994, my mother made her transition from life experience to what lies beyond it. She died about two months shy of her 78th birthday.

In addition to beginning a grief and mourning process, my family and I also reached for joy as much as possible considering our loss. There were two main reasons why we tried to focus on celebration through our bereavement.

The first reason had to do with the 77+ years that my mother lived. The second was related to our collective belief about what lies beyond the grave. We are among the ever-increasing number of people who believe that there is "life after life."

Some years ago, Leo Buscaglia wrote a wonderful addition to his series of thoughtful books called <u>Living, Loving, and Learning</u>. In my mind, the title of his book sums up the entire purpose of our existence; but a great deal of the literature on both life (and afterlife) experiences also supports this view.

If, indeed, living, loving and learning are our core purposes for existing in the world, my mother did a beautiful job of focusing on all three. Hazel Simon lived every day vibrantly. Diabetes claimed one of her legs and some of her physical strength years ago, but her spirit was indomitable. From a wheelchair, she cooked, did laundry, cleaned her house, cared for my father and (at times) two to six grandchildren, and did all of her own lawn care except for mowing.

My mother had a wonderful sense of fun and humor. On her last day, through pain and discomfort, she grinned and joked with two nurses that she knew them but didn't know my sister (who was present at the time and played "straight man" for the joke.)

My mother definitely lived every day of her life. She didn't ask for much and seldom complained. She sometimes had a habit of wishing out loud for which we are eternally grateful. That was usually the best way for us to learn about her needs.

But as much as (or more) than my mother lived, she also loved. She had a keen sense of right and wrong and strongly disliked (maybe even hated) behaviors in people and groups that were not honorable. But apart from that, her whole life was motivated by her love—for my father, for her children and grandchildren, and for anyone else who needed it (whether they knew they needed it or not.)

My mother was also a lover of learning, and she transferred that love to her children. Like many people, she was not always quick to embrace new ideas; but she was always open to them. She developed a love for reading as a schoolgirl that followed her throughout her life. She looked at problems as challenges and met them with much the same exuberance that she attacked the jigsaw and word search puzzles that she dearly loved.

Living, loving and learning. I have had wonderful models of the value of pursuing these life purposes in both of my parents. They taught me by example to embrace life with its many vicissitudes and to always meet its challenges with my best effort. They taught me the insuperable value of loving everyone and the incredible power that comes from learning all you can learn. I could never be persuaded that these are not our supreme purposes in life.

If there were ever any doubt in my mind, it would not be likely to survive in light of the evidence that is presented in books like the New York Times bestseller Embraced By The Light by Betty J. Eadie. Increasingly, people who report experiences beyond the confines of the body also report that—in their interactions with other entities—they are somehow held accountable for how they lived, how they loved, and how they learned.

From a consultant named Miriam Black, I picked up a formula that has been very helpful in encouraging me (and others with whom I've shared it) to keep a healthy perspective about the experiences of life. The formula is **E + R = O** and is translated as **Events + Responses = Outcomes**.

In the final analysis, we have varying degrees of control of the events of our lives, but we almost always have control of our responses to the events. If we respond by tenaciously embracing life, love, and learning, positive and joyous outcomes are assured.

CHANNEL

Channel—
Open conduit from There to Here;
A means by which my mind understands the
    Incomprehensible;
A link from mind to heart to God and back;
A lens through which my mind's eye sees
    Into the unknown.

Channel—
Tuned in to the sights and sounds of the universe—
    One by one, or all together;
Hot-line to Pure Energy;
A way to travel across the space of time or
    Across the time of space;
The thread that ties me to my brother, my sister,
    And you.

Channel—
The airwave that makes of me an empath
    Who knows your joy and feels your pain;
That which makes of me a source of good in the world
    Through actions...or mere thought alone;
That part of me which defies description,
    Resists location,
        Escapes my vision,
            Is in no way tactile
But ultimately connects me
To everything.
Channel—
One of many of the fundamental divisions of
Tele-Everything and
    Auto-Everything and
        Everything I ought to know and tell
            But don't or can't because
I haven't learned to access the right
Channel.

WHEN WE ASSUME ABOUT EACH OTHER
(THE DANGER OF TAKING ANYTHING FOR GRANTED)

Sometimes, it's amazing what we will do for the sake of convenience in relationships and interactions with others. From encounters with strangers, to connections with those with whom we are most intimately involved, we occasionally short-circuit the process of true acquaintance in favor of unreasonable facsimiles thereof.

One of the biggest culprits, in this case, is assumption. We sometimes take clues from occurrences, or the behaviors of people, and assume certainties about who or what they are. Sometimes we even make assertions with no external clues at all. We take something for granted or suppose something to be a fact when the fact is, what we suppose is only what we suppose.

Of course, this is not much of a problem if we happen to be right. But it can be a real problem when we turn out to be wrong. And as Murphy would have it, if we can be wrong, we will—and likely more often than we are not.

How do we develop the habit of making assumptions about each other when it is often just as easy to clarify with questions? Why do we often display an accusatory tone in what we choose to say or ask when an inquisitive one would work just as well? Why do we not only make our assumptions but also act on them as if they were already proven true with overwhelming evidence?

I wish I knew the answers to these questions. I have some ideas, but I recognize them for what they are…assumptions. I <u>assume</u>, for example, that most of us are more egocentric than we like to think we are. As a result, we often attribute motivations to others that we believe <u>we</u> would have under similar circumstances. And to compound the matter, we are often not even <u>certain</u> of what we <u>would</u> do under the same or similar circumstances.

I <u>assume</u> that we choose an accusatory tone when we act on our assumptions because we have seen that tactic modeled much more often than the simple and respectful questioning tone. On top of that, we have been the <u>accused</u> ones so often that a deep-rooted (if not substantial) pain may fuel what is almost an entirely reflexive retaliation.

Finally, I think we <u>make</u> our assumptions and then <u>act</u> on them as if they were already proven true because we're too lazy, or too hurried, or too insensitive to seek out the evidence that would support or indict the assumption. The extra effort is too inconvenient.

Of course, I could be completely wrong. After all, I'm only making assumptions based on <u>my</u> perspective. I don't, for a minute, assume that you agree with me. But if you are, at least, <u>thinking</u> about how assumptions play a part in <u>your</u> experience, you can make your own determinations about <u>why</u> and devise your <u>own</u> strategy for minimizing the potential for damage done.

Often becoming aware of a foible is more than half the battle in an effort to make positive personal change. If we could assume less and question more, it would be helpful for us all. But then again, that's just what I assume. Yet maybe this is one where I'm right. I will invite that possibility with cautious optimism.

SERENDIPITY?
(DOES ANYTHING EVER REALLY HAPPEN BY ACCIDENT?)

There is a story I'd like to read someday...if it exists in print. You see, I've only heard about it. I've never seen a copy, and I've never talked to anyone who confesses having ever read it. Apparently, however, there is a book (or at least a story) called <u>The Three Princes of Serendip.</u> It is said that this story is the source of the word serendipity.

In fact, if you look up the word "serendipity" in the dictionary, you may learn that Horace Walpole coined the term. Good, old Horace is described in my handy, dandy encyclopedia as an "English letter writer, historian, connoisseur, and amateur architect" who died at age 80 in 1797. There are many interesting tidbits about Walpole (such as the fact that he might be called "The Father of Gothic Romance") but we will concentrate on the fact that <u>he</u> <u>gave</u> us the word serendipity, which roughly means "a happy accident."

<u>The Three Princes of Serendip</u> is a Persian fairy tale, which centers around three lucky guys who have a knack for finding good fortune purely by accident. I guess a <u>modern</u>-day version of this story might be Forrest Gump. Now <u>there's</u> an example of someone who almost always seemed to be in the right place, at the right time, doing the right thing. Lucky is as lucky does, I guess. For Forrest, it worked out that way...even though he understood (and helped us to understand) how "life is like a box of chocolates; you never know what you're gonna get."

What I'd like us to think about is whether or not there really are "happy accidents." Actually, the better question is, "Is there any such thing as an accident at all?" There are people who say (and I think I'm one of them) that there is no such thing as an accident; that everything happens by design. It may be a personal design, an evil design, a grand design, or a Divine design, but every occurrence has a purpose, a rhyme and reason.

Viewed in this light, maybe serendipity's definition should be changed. But if it should, what will we change it to? If things that seem to happen by accident really aren't happenstance at all, maybe we could call them GMC's. That's what Helen Durbin called them.

Helen Durbin, among other things was the wife of a former director of the Kansas State High School Activities Association and quite a lady, in my opinion. It was she who introduced me to the idea of a GMC—which is not an automobile. For her, the apparent surprises of life were not accidents, but God-Made Coincidences...GMC's...instead.

Perhaps we can take a cue from James Redfield and really try to fathom the meaning behind our twists of fate and turns of fortune. At the beginning of his popular story The Celestine Prophecy, a character named Charlene declares, "...these *coincidences* are happening more and more frequently and...when they do, they strike us as beyond what would be expected by pure chance. They feel destined, as though some unexplained force had guided our lives. The experience induces a feeling of mystery and excitement and, as a result, we feel more alive."

Redfield also says—through Charlene—that what is really important is that we become *conscious* of the coincidences in our lives. So pause for a moment, and consider whether or not you are conscious of these serendipitous events in your life.

What gifts do your coincidences contribute to you? How much happiness is there in your happenstance? What good can be gleaned from the misery of your mishaps? How much serenity can be sifted from your serendipitous, social encounters? What lessons can be learned from your lamentations on lucklessness?

In other words, if you carefully observed the past, present and penultimate pieces of your life, what meaningful pattern would be produced for your perusal and appreciation? The chances are good that an intricate and fabulous mosaic would marvelously emerge!

LIFE IMITATES ART!
(A 180-DEGREE TWIST ON AN OLD TRUISM)

How often life imitates art!
If you notice something peculiar about this statement, you don't have to pinch yourself to see if you're still dreaming. You really are awake and you read it right. I deliberately blasphemed the point of view of the famous Elizabethan bard. I'm just struck with how true this reversal of the well-known exclamation really is.

Life really does imitate art. I think it always has. But because of the influence of modern recorded music, videos, movies, television and a host of other art forms that are more or less synonymous with mass communication, the incidence of life imitating the artist's conception is even more prevalent.

Sometimes the imitations are not very accurate, however. For example, I remember when the rock group Pink Floyd released their album "Another Brick In The Wall." Whenever I was around kids listening to the title cut, you can bet they all lustily sang the first line of the song, which is "We don't need no education." I suspect there were quite a few of them, though, who never listened carefully enough to the rest of the song. If they had, they would have known the song was really speaking out against things like "thought control" and "dark sarcasm in the classroom." I vote for both of those.

In recent times, how often did you hear someone jokingly (or seriously) say, "I love you, man!"? In my experience, I have regularly witnessed this phrase being used in light conversation after it was introduced in a fairly popular light beer commercial—especially with kids. (I also have to wonder at the kind of desperation displayed in the commercials. Unfortunately, for most people, that element is probably easily overlooked in the process of enjoying the character. But that's another story.)

And speaking of kids, I hardly ever saw any of them do what they call "head-banging" while listening to rock music until it was popularized by the "Beavis and Butthead" phenomenon. And the baggy clothing style called "saggin'" wasn't a fashion statement until rap artists began to costume that way.

Not very long ago, I recall that there were current dance crazes called the "Smurf" and the "Roger Rabbit." Cartoon characters, of course, inspired both of these. Cartoon features have given us songs regularly performed at weddings. They have given us voice characterizations often imitated for fun...and profit.

My son used to have a friend in our old neighborhood that would sometime call when we were out and leave a message on the answering machine. On separate occasions, I heard him do fair imitations of Clint Eastwood, Arnold Schwarzenegger, and James Cagney. James Cagney? Either this kid has watched quite a few old movies, or (as is just as likely the case) he has picked up the characterization from a cartoon villain modeled after the gangsters interpreted by Cagney and Edward G. Robinson and others years ago.

Valley girls would probably still be in The Valley if it were not for mass media. Instead, "valley-speak" shows up from coast to coast and beyond. Jim Carrey's Ace Ventura pops up in a lot of places, too. "Well, alrighty then!"

Thanks to Dana Carvey, Eddie Murphy, and others, we have also learned to do voice caricatures of public figures such as Presidents Reagan, Bush, Nixon, Carter and Clinton as well as folks like Martin Luther King, Jr., Jesse Jackson, and the Love Maestro, Barry White.

We were once taught by a commercial to ask, "Is it live or is it Memorex?" Nowadays, when it comes to what we are living, we have to ask, "Is it life, or is it art?"

THE BAND-AID ADVENTURE
("IT WON'T HURT A BIT!")

If I mention "Band-Aid" and "body hair" in the same sentence, does it make you cringe? If it does, then you probably remember a childhood experience like one of mine.

I can't remember for sure if this little experience happened with one of my parents or with our family doctor; but either way, I had a learning experience that I'm certain I would not have chosen if I had had a choice. Fortunately, I didn't.

The essence of the story is this: I had experienced a minor injury of some sort that required a bandage. A specimen of the common, adhesive backed variety was applied. In due time, it had to be removed. At the moment of truth, I recalled previous experiences where such removal had felt as though my entire skin was being ripped off—either all at once, or with agonizing, torturous slowness. Naturally, I was quite apprehensive at the prospect.

I decided to be as assertive as I knew how at that moment. As the caring adult reached to pinch a leading edge of the covering on my wound, I sobbed, "It's going to hurt!" The adult calmly replied, "Oh, it's not going to hurt that much!" And just as the word "much" was uttered, the bandage came off in one fell swoop. It hurt, of course, but the sensation was short-lived, the pain was negligible, and any damage to my person was quite minimal.

I also discovered that my anticipation of the pain was worse than the pain itself. That was the first of two parts of the lesson. The second part came as I had similar experiences at later times. When it was time for the bandage to be removed on these occasions, I steeled myself by remembering how I survived my previous experiences and anticipated each subsequent one with far less dread. In fact, you might say I embraced the occurrences instead. Sure enough, the discomfort was there each time but was of short duration and usually had no lasting repercussions.

What I have unearthed in the blur of years since then is that what I call the "Lesson of the Band-Aid" has found translations in a number of other experiences where the endurance of pain is a possibility. Often the anticipation of the pain is worse than the actuality. Usually, my ability to endure it is quite adequate. I have survived them all, so far, and witnessed survivals by others of painful happenings that seem far more intense than my own. And this has been true for me and for others even when the hurt has been worse than imagined in advance.

This understanding is part of the reason why I continue to learn in more and more ways to embrace my experiences no matter what they may be; for they all have meaning; and they are all a part of the flow of life that is necessary for us. To have the unique experience that we are destined to have, to learn the lessons we must learn, and to grow in the ways we must each grow, we should remember the "Lesson of the Band-Aid."

WHEN YOUR "GET UP AND GO" GETS UP AND GOES
(HONORING LIFE'S RHYTHMS)

When I was a kid growing up, my dad was well-known in our intimate world for casually tossing little tidbits of humor into everyday conversation. I don't know that we ever had a clue how he acquired these little gems; but just about the time we would get used to hearing one, he'd come up with another that we hadn't heard.

I thought about one of dad's little goodies when I got up feeling tired recently. If someone asked my dad how <u>he</u> was feeling at a time when fatigue was present, they might hear him jokingly reply with a disarming, deadpan expression and intentional bad grammar, "I think my get-up-and-go done got up and went!"

Expressions like that would leave us momentarily stuck in limbo somewhere between a laugh and genuine confusion. Eventually this would generally give way to mild disgust (when we knew we had been had again) and a smile or a chuckle shared with our "silly" dad.

Sometimes, though, your get-up-and-go <u>does</u> get up and go...somewhere. It may be due to illness, or fatigue, or injury on some occasions; but at other times, the cause for that draggy feeling is a mystery.

In my efforts to be more intuitive in my life, I try to pay attention to mysterious fatigue. What I find is that there is usually a message in that for me; and if the cause of my weariness is not readily apparent, I try to slow my pace, concentrate on what I'm feeling, and find a different rhythm.

I find that personal energies, for me, are like prevailing winds that seem to be almost always available. I catch them in the sails of my intentions and use them in propelling myself forward to my goals. But there are days when there seems to be little or no wind available.

On some of these days, it seems like the smartest thing to do is to just wait until the wind picks up rather than to put my oars in the water and row when I'm already tired. On other days, no matter how tired I feel, it makes more sense to row rather than lose the momentum of my forward motion. As always, though, the dilemma is to determine which days are which.

Science and philosophy have discovered and defined for us that life is rhythmic; it is cyclical; it is prone to ups and downs, to vicissitudes; it moves in wavelike patterns; it ebbs and flows. It behooves us to understand that; but once we accept that, our next task is to determine how to deal with it. Do we row, or wait for favorable winds?

There is no easy answer for any of us when our personal energies have ebbed; but that's okay. What we need more than an easy answer is an easy question; and that's available. The question is, "What does this mean?"

Remember to ask that question whenever you can claim that your get-up-and-go got up and went; but also remember to expect to get an answer and to be patient about getting it. For like the winds of energy we depend on, our answers do not always come with gale-like force. Instead, they may be whispered to us on a barely perceptible breeze that gently tickles the spiritual inner ear which can hear the inner voice.

Make sure you are listening carefully.

THE NEW A.M.N.E.S.I.A.
(AN UNOFFICIAL GROUP WE'D ALL LIKE TO FORGET)

There is a brand-new organization in America starting as of this moment. Its charter is imbedded within the words that follow. However, there are already people who are founding members of the group (whether they know it or acknowledge it or not); but I sincerely hope you are not one of them.

The new organization is called the **AM**erican **NE**ophyte **S**ociety of **I**gnorance and **A**pathy (or AMNESIA.) Their motto is, "We don't know, and we don't care." Members are generally called Amnesians, but those in the lunatic fringe of the group are called Amnesi*acs* because their dedication to ignorance and apathy is so intense that they are considered maniacs compared to the rest of the group.

Neophyte is part of the organization's name because all members must be newly converted to the group each day. As the wealth of information available and the need to be informed increases among the general population; and as the realization of the power of cooperation and collaboration grows in society; members of AMNESIA have to constantly discover or create new ways to not know and not care.

There are other branches of the organization worldwide. These include the European arm, EUNESIA (they're called the "Yoonies") and the Asian offshoot ASNESIA where members are called "Sneezies." There is even an Australian chapter—AUNESIA—that sports members who call themselves the "Aunties." But nowhere is the dedication to lack of knowledge and lack of compassion any more prevalent than among the members of the American group.

The Amnesians pride themselves on not knowing about a lot of things. They don't know about cultures other than their own. They don't know about self-empowerment. They don't know about media bias and influence. They don't know how minds work, how bodies work, how schools work, how businesses work, how governments work, or how economies work. Among the leadership of the group, it is even sometimes true that they don't know that they don't know! And, of course, they don't care.

The greatest claim to notoriety for Amnesians and their kin, though, may be their amazing ability to not care. They don't care about elections. They don't care about diets. They don't care about exercising their bodies OR their minds. They don't care about the environment. They don't care about learning. They don't care about religion or spirituality. They don't care about anything except MAYBE themselves. And most of all they don't care about not caring about anything other than themselves...if they even care about that. The Amnesiacs are well known for this particular aspect.

I suppose you can see now why I'm really hoping you're not an Amnesian. Obviously, people who continue to embrace unawareness and indifference will be of little use to the rest of us and in danger of becoming extinct themselves. And yet the organization seems to attract new members daily.

Perhaps we should charter another organization. We could call it **A.L.A.R.M.I.S.T.**, The **A**merican **L**eague of **A**ction to **R**equire **M**assive **I**nformation **S**ensitivity and **T**olerance. That ought to wake up the Amnesians, don't you think? After all, there may be a lot that folks don't know, but they sure as heck need to care. Our survival may depend on it.

HOW TO LOVE A HATER
(AN ADVANCED PRIMER FOR GETTING ALONG)

ll right, class; today's lesson is, "How To Love a Hater." Yes, you heard me right. How to <u>love</u> a <u>hater</u>! Now, I know you think that's an obvious contradiction in terms; oxymoronic, at best; the acme of stupidity, at the worst. Ah, but therein lie the beauty and the challenge of the whole thing. When you know <u>how</u> to <u>do</u> it, the contradiction disappears, the oxymoron disintegrates, and the perception of stupidity evaporates.

You see, it's a "Catch 21." It's not quite a Catch 22. The situation is not nearly as challenging as not being able to get a job because you have no experience, and not being able to get experience because you can't get a job. It's not even as tough as trying to figure out whether the chicken or the egg came first. No sir-ee, this one is much simpler.

Loving a hater starts off with understanding what a "hater" is. A hater is a person who is ill. Really. Haters have a sickness inside that makes them rant and rave and speak absurdities. It contorts their facial features, and tightens most of the muscles in their bodies whenever they consider the objects of their hatefulness. It causes them to be violent and abusive. It steals days from their lives because time spent hating is always lost. Hate is also a chronic and progressive disease that is terminal if it goes untreated.

The disease of hate is caused by several pathogens. The major of these is a virus called fear. If you dig deep enough below the surface of hate, you will often find something that the hater is afraid of. Usually, it will be the loss (or the imagined or anticipated loss) of something they don't own or have a right to in the first place. But sometimes, what they fear most is that they will look inside themselves and find an empty void. What they don't know, however, is that this fear, itself, creates the emptiness they fear. That's a Catch 21.5

For many who are not incapacitated by the virus of fear, there is a bacterium called ignorance that often induces the hater's disease. This is a terrible cause of the malady of hate because ignorance usually breeds more ignorance by setting up antibodies to learning. Hate often thrives where facts are lacking and worsens where they are not sought.

The third leading cause of hate is a germ called frustration. This is a difficult diagnosis because the germ often disguises itself (among other things) as anger, revengefulness, retaliation, powerlessness, AND ignorance…especially ignorance of self.

But now, here's the moment you have been waiting for! How do you love a hater? The same way you would love someone who has the flu, or cancer, or arthritis, or Alzheimer's, or AIDS. You don't hate someone who is sick; you just "hate" (so to speak) the illness. You just try to help them or see that they get help from someone who can help if you can't.

Of course, there is always the sick person who seems to love their illness and who apparently doesn't want to get well. But we don't stop loving them either. We just choose to do it from a distance. So if a hateful person won't let you love them close up, just do it from far away. Zap them with prayer or positive thoughts. They won't know what hit them; and unless you tell them, they won't know whom. But you'll know whom, and you'll know why, because now you know how.

ABOVE THE CLOUDS
(THE POWER OF PERSPECTIVE PLUS...)

In the work I do with young student audiences, I sometimes ask the question, "How many of you know that everyday of your life, the sun has been shining and the sky has been blue?" Almost immediately I see quizzical looks on many of the faces which seem to indicate the widespread conclusion that I have taken leave of my senses.

If I'm really lucky, it will be a cloudy day when I pop this question; and if windows are available, heads will turn for a moment to check the current reality and then back to me. By that time, I'm probably saying something like, "If you don't believe me, all you have to do is pick any cloudy day and take an airplane ride up above the clouds and you'll see that I'm right. The sun is shining and the sky is blue. You may not always be able to see it from where you are, but it's always true."

At this point, I often watch new little lights pop on behind the eyes of certain heads around the room, and I feel like I've helped to add a few more lumens to the brilliance of some young awarenesses. I generally continue my talk with some discussion of the power of perspective...and imagination. It's a lesson that's worth repeating—not only for the sake of the learners, but also for the teacher.

Of course, if I'm really being ornery, I'll haul off and hit 'em with one of the favorite greetings of my friend, Tim. Sometimes when I greet him with the classic greeting query of, "How are you?" he'll reply with, "I've never had a bad day in my life." Of course, I happen to know that if there were such a thing as a "Bad Day Meter," Tim has lived through some days that would break the indicator needles for a lot of people. But I know Tim; and he's not just being flip. It's about perspective...and attitude. As my favorite Zen

Buddhist illustration says about vicissitudes of life, "It's not a good thing; it's not a bad thing; it just is what it is." Or as Les Brown puts it, "Any day above ground is a good day."

And now, as streams of consciousness tend to do, this one makes me think of Sir Isaac Newton and other pioneers of physics who helped us understand concepts like, "What goes up, must come down;" and "For every action, there is an equal and opposite reaction;" or they have invited us to ponder the conundrum of what would happen if an irresistible force meets an immovable object. This, of course, is about perspective.... and balance.

But on the other hand, any projectile that we blast beyond earth's orbit into the weightlessness of space is not likely to ever come down again—at least not here. And on cloudy days, airplane rides and imagination won't keep sunflowers from drooping or certain sun worshipers from losing their natural tans. And sometimes, the days of our lives are more tragic than we can manage easily, or without help. But this, too, is about perspective...and maybe...chaos.

Given a choice, though, I'd rather remember that the clouds and storms of life only obscure the larger reality that sunshine and blue skies are the way of this world. In fact, if it weren't for the latter we wouldn't have the other...which makes me think of cycles. Sunshine... evaporation... cloudy skies... precipitation... and then the same thing all over again. Perspective... imagination... attitude... balance... chaos... cycles... paradoxes... all part of the fascinating world we can observe from a lofty perspective above the clouds...maybe on a stormy day...with bright, blue skies.

CHASING HUNCHES
(LEARNING TO LIVE WELL WITH INTUITION)

On a particular quiet morning, two friends popped into my mind without warning, and for no apparent reason. Usually when that happens, even though the reasons are not apparent, I figure explanations are bubbling right below the surface of my awareness. In other words, if someone or something comes to mind, I know something's up. I'm learning that it's sometimes productive to entertain the next thought that comes to mind ...if possible.

So... on this particular morning, I pick up the phone and dial numbers for the two friends. I get an answering machine for the first one. The second friend is in the bath when I call, and I leave a message with one of her children. Sounds like strike one and strike two, right? Wrong!

It turns out that the first friend had decided to sleep in, but returns my call later. We have a very nice chat. And the second one? At the end of the day I ask her if she got the message that I called just to tell her I love her. She says, "You don't KNOW how much that meant to me. It made me feel I could go on with my day." Well, whaddaya know? Two home runs instead!

So how did that happen? Simple... (or maybe not so simple.) Intuition came fishing for me, and I took the bait. You know, they say you have to be careful what you ask for because you just might get it. Well, I've been saying I want to learn to recognize and trust my intuition more, and by Jiminy, there are times when I think it's coming along!

Consider this. I'm preparing a very simple dinner for my family one evening. I have one vegetable, bread, and a deli-roasted chicken. I think to myself, "It sure would be nice to add one more vegetable...a green one. For a moment, I eye a jar of pickles wistfully but decide that's stretching it a little. Ten minutes later, my son is serving himself what I've prepared and what does he decide to add to his plate? A dill spear! So I place the jar on the table while my wife is eating and suggest she take one, and she does! I'm not so nuts after all.

On another occasion, I'm driving to rendezvous with my family and suddenly remember that my mobile phone is not on. I press the power button and ten seconds later the phone rings. It's my wife sharing corrected directions that save me a wild goose chase on the way to our meeting.

Once, over a period of several days, I thought of a friend repeatedly… but thought I <u>shouldn't</u> call, so I didn't. It's just as well. She was out of town anyway.

Sudden thoughts of another friend on <u>one</u> day heralded a postcard which came the <u>following</u> day. A spontaneous visit to another friend allowed me to discover that he had just experienced a death in his family. And for still another friend, I postponed a proposition for him a day longer than I knew I should only to find that someone else had made the same offer earlier on the day I finally got around to it.

It's a strange and wonderful thing, this thing called intuition. It may lead one to do something, or to not do something, to wait, to visit, to pray, to call, to move, to stay still, to send mental thoughts of love. Learning to know which is which and when is when is exciting stuff…especially when you get it right!

WEE HOUR MEDITATION

A half-moon sat
In the Southern sky
Like a white, China teacup
Tipped
For the last sip.

Stars were a handful of rhinestones
Scattered across
A midnight blue tablecloth.

The night blanketed me
In layers of chilled air.

The quiet was awesome—
My breaths the only breeze,
My heartbeats like native drums
Punctuating the dark serenity.

Alone with my thoughts,
I contemplated the vastness
Of my own mind,
And how comfortably it rests
In the spaciousness
Of God's.

How like the sun God is!!
That great ball of fire
That greets us daily
Is far too gigantic
To be contained on the Earth;
Yet its brilliance
Creeps into every space—
Every crack and crevice
That opens to the light.

So, too, is God—
Magnificently apart from us,
Pervasively a part of us.

I considered that in the crisp night
And was warmed by the thought
Sunshine can't be trapped
in a clay pot
And dumped out
On unsuspecting darkness,
But God can.

We are clay pots
Where God can be stored
And allowed
To radiate
Anywhere,
Everywhere,
Anytime,
All the time...
To erase the darkness of our souls.

I reflected
And smiled
As the rhinestone stars
Slowly vanished
From the night-sky tablecloth,
And the teacup moon
Began to fade
In the quiet, gray light
Of dawn.

COSMIC TOYS: BATTERY POWERED

(A MEDITATION ON THE RELATIONSHIP OF "GOD" TO "MAN")

When the term "god" emerges in human awareness (for whatever reason and in whatever particular way) it invokes thoughts, feelings and actions that become a veritable potpourri when the diversity of the world's population comes into play. And when the designation is "God" with a capital "G," meaning an absolutely supreme being, the debate about the existence or nature of such a God can be vehement.

Needless to say, I'm part of this on-going and universal dialogue about ultimate spiritual powers in the Universe; and I don't mind going on record with a perspective.

In fact, while in search of an analogy that might help to explain our relationship as humans to a Supreme God, electricity and its relationship to battery-powered machines came to mind for me. And whether this view is right or wrong or shared by others or not, it sure is fun to consider it.

But first, let me say that I believe that there is a Supreme Being in the Universe which out-ranks every other entity or power. God (with a capital "G") is both the term and the name I choose to use for this Being, but I have no problem with people who have different perceptions.

Atheists say there is no God, and Agnostics say the human mind is incapable of knowing whether there is a God or not. Believers say there is a God but they either know this intuitively, by faith, or because they have in some way had a personal experience with God, as they understand God.

Regardless of which camp we're in, I don't think any of us can prove those in the other camps right or wrong—at least not scientifically. I believe we are each left, as always, with the need to make these determinations for ourselves. We can only hope (in the absence of definitive proof) that our perspective is accurate; or if it is not, that it is, at least, supported and affirmed by a significant number of others who share it. I suppose error can love company as much as misery.

I think of God as the ultimate power or energy behind every element of the universe. To me, God is like spiritual electricity that empowers everyone and everything.

I sometimes refer to God as "He" for convenience or out of the habit of tradition. But most times I simply say "God" (as I have so far in this commentary) and avoid personal pronouns that limit a limitless (and genderless) God. In fact, I believe that any idea of God limits God. In my opinion, God is beyond ideas; and yet, our ideas of God are what allow us to relate to God Him-, Her- or Itself.

But if God is the "Ultimate Electricity" that energizes the Universe, then we are like battery-powered toys or machines. We exist for some specific purpose or purposes and are inherently capable of performing alone for most of those purposes. But for those necessary or desirable functions that are beyond the scope of our battery's power, an adapter allows us to "plug in" to the Ultimate Electricity for the power we need.

When we need extra power or to recharge our batteries, we do so through prayer and meditation, or by exercising our faith like a generator. When our batteries can no longer recharge, and our generator cannot produce life's energy, we expire; we cease to function in ways we are used to. But unlike machines, our ultimate ability to function apparently does not expire. There is a part of us that can somehow exist and operate apart from what we know as our normal abilities. Perhaps it's like a computerized component in a machine that can be removed and used even when the rest of the machine is useless. Or perhaps the analogy falls short of perfect here.

Nevertheless, God (as I choose to conceive God) is the ENERGY of All Energies, the SOUL of All Souls, the SPIRIT of All Spirits, the LOVE of All Loves, the POWER of All Powers, the KNOWING of All Knowings, the LIFE of All Life…and perhaps the PARADOX of All Paradoxes.

If an Omniscient, Omnipotent, Omni-Present God exists beyond our ability to perceive such a God, the question is, "How can we ever truly know that such a God exists?" How can we see a God who can see everything when our ability to perceive falls short of that? How can we know a God who knows everything when we know so little? How can we meet Ultimate Power when intimacy with some of the powers we do know would destroy us? How can we put ourselves in a place to view an omni-present God without ourselves being Omni-Present?

Perhaps we can only investigate available evidence and make inferences about God from that. But for this battery-powered device, that's enough.

A MATTER OF SPIRIT

Do you ever wish you could move through your experience with your feet floating above the ground?

Do you ever wish that you were invulnerable and that you could laugh at the things that hurt you most?

Do you ever wish that you could simply observe the humdrum or the storms of life as if they were on television rather than be caught up in them?

Do you ever stop to consider the significance of the fact that part of you is capable of all of that and more?

There is a formless, shapeless, timeless, colorless, tasteless, odorless essence of who you are that remains somehow blissfully independent of every single circumstance of your life. It's the part of you called spirit or soul.

Webster does not differentiate a great deal between spirit and soul. In fact the terms are regarded more or less as synonymous. In the first sense, "soul" is defined, in part, as "an entity which is regarded as being the immortal or spiritual part of the person" while the first entry of the definition of "spirit" ends by calling it the "same as soul."

On the other hand, in the book Soul Mates, author Thomas Moore does make a distinction. He writes, for example, that "It's important to… be free of everyday worldly concerns in order to explore fully the realm of spirit…. But the soul has an equal task and commitment, to find the treasures and explore the ins and outs of life by being attached. Just as there is spiritual practice in search of the highest and most refined reaches of human potential, so there is soul practice in pursuit of the juices and nutriments of life's entanglements."

Gary Zukav writes similarly in The Seat Of The Soul. He says, "Spirituality has to do with the immortal process itself...[It] is not limited to your personality and its intuitional system. [It] encompasses your whole soul's journey, whereas your intuition is the way that your soul can contact your beingness to help it in [various] situations. ...when you leave your body, the intuitional system that was developed for that body will be left behind because it will no longer be necessary."

In my mind, we are being invited by both of these thinkers to involve ourselves in an on-going process to clarify our perspectives on and our approaches to our life experiences. As we move through our lives and encounter our lives' events, perhaps we should ask ourselves how the events matter. In other words, we should ask if each event is a matter of soul, or if it is a matter of spirit. There can be no question about whether or not it does matter. Everything matters. Questions about how things matter simply help us to clarify a perspective that can help us respond effectively.

The problem for most of us is that we get caught up in matter itself, in physicality, in objects, in circumstances, in reality as we perceive it through the physical senses. Somehow, matter becomes more real and more important to us than soul or spirit. Is it because we neglect to recognize the credentials of spirit or soul while we're trapped in the clay?

Looked at another way, if life is like a huge ocean, some of us are so overwhelmed by its vastness that we make ourselves content to wade along the shore and collect the trinkets that are washed up by its ebb and flow. We are frightened by its size, its power, and its coldness and may feel as powerless to move away from it as we do to engage it. If so, then we are the ones who share perspectives that are at the level of matter. We most often simply allow life to happen to us, suffer the consequences, and complain about unfairness and injustice.

At the level of soul, though, we are the ones who learn ways to swim and ski and scuba dive through the waters of life. We build fishing boats and submarines and sailing clippers and ocean liners and allow our experiences with the ocean of life to teach us about the ocean itself and about ourselves. We embrace all of our experiences and refrain from judging them good or bad but simply as experiences that are important to help us understand and manage life itself.

From the spiritual viewpoint, we learn to recognize that the waters of life are often subject to our will. We also learn that just because we can master the ocean doesn't mean that we should. We begin to understand that each event that happens in the waters requires a unique response.

Sometimes we may need to wave our arms over the water and part the seas, or choose to run across the tops of the waves rather than swim. At other times, we may need to don our scuba gear and dive to the depths to encounter and vanquish frightening sea monsters. Then again, sudden storms may arise on the ocean and engulf us with circumstances that leave us no choice but to deal with the "matter" of it all.

But should our bodies not be destroyed by life's unpleasant surprises, we will soon have another opportunity to reach for either the mundane tools, or the more powerful ones of soul or spirit.

THE CONTENT OF SPIRIT
(WHAT'S IN THE VESSEL WITHIN THE VESSEL)

We have shared a bit about the more nebulous aspects of who we are as conscious, perceptive human beings alive on planet earth. We have engaged in a somewhat esoteric exploration of the distinctions that might be made between those parts of us called "spirit" and "soul." We have recognized that even though many regard the two terms as synonymous, a convincing case can be made for thinking of them differently.

Although Webster's first entry in the definition of the term "spirit" ends by calling it the "same as soul," reading further into its long defining passage allows us to discover meanings expressed in ways that perhaps belie the synonym.

Spirit is defined as "the thinking, motivating, feeling part of man," or "life, will, consciousness, or thought." Spirit is also the term, which conveys the meaning "a super-natural being," which, in turn, means one that "exists or occurs outside of the normal experience or knowledge of man." Ultimately, spirit is an essence that pervades our entire experience as we know it. It is also the foundation of experiences that we currently have no way of knowing—even in the rather limited way that we know our own.

When Thomas Moore writes that spiritual practice is the search for the highest and most refined reaches of human potential and Gary Zukav adds that it is not limited to our personalities and their intuitional systems but encompasses our whole soul's journey, these descriptions instantly take us far beyond the superficial.

If, as Thomas Moore writes, "there is soul practice in pursuit of the juices and nutriments of life's entanglements," then spiritual practice is what allows us to conceive of what to do with those juices and nutriments when we are able to extract them from our experience.

In my mind, "spirit" is the realm of consciousness, perception, ideas, creative energy, vision, dreams, art, music, love, healing, enlightenment and more. As a place to begin, however, this list is more than enough for us to consider as we ponder that "spirit" is an indelible element of who we are.

To say that we are spiritual beings is to invoke potentials that are so awesome as to be, in some ways, unbelievable. Yet, our inability to <u>appreciate</u> the incredible nature of these possibilities is also, unfortunately, at the root of a huge problem. We get so caught up in the entanglements of life that we forget that we are endowed with a spirit that is supernatural, that "exists or occurs outside of the normal experience or knowledge of man."

The key here is that we often have to get outside of our normal experience in order to access the fruits of spirit. Perhaps this means we have to occasionally be abnormal, or paranormal, or supernormal, or even anti-normal in order to traverse the world of spirit. In some ways, we have to be extraordinary, irregular, above average, unusual, atypical, and nonconforming for spirit to speak to us or through us.

What is normal, what is standard, what is average, what is ordinary, what is usual or typical, is that most of us have come to believe in ourselves as beings with far less ability than we really have. But it is only when we reach out for more of what is latent within us that we find it.

Fortunately, some of us allow ourselves to discover big chunks of our potential and then we become models for others. Unfortunately, others of us mistake these models for paragons of perfection or excellence that are meant only to inspire us to become marvels ourselves! In fact, we should imitate the successful recipes of the exemplars we admire, incorporate their ideas into our original designs, or simply initiate searches for our own undiscovered gifts!

Spirit is the realm of full consciousness; we need to make an effort to wake up to more and more of what is dormant in us. Spirit is the realm of accurate perception; we need to learn to see the things we think we already know in new lights.

Spirit is the world of ideas, visions, and dreams. We must learn not to fear or discount what appears in our awareness. We could well be viewing prototypes for constructs that are emerging from the blueprint of the world we are always in the process of helping to shape—either consciously or blindly.

Spirit is a universe filled with the creative energy that gives birth to the ever-broadening worlds of art, music, love, healing, and enlightenment.

The doorway to these worlds within worlds is inside of each of us. It's called spirit; and the key to the door is also in our possession. It's called belief. Believe in the power of the spirit within you and your experience will flower.

PRAYING TOGETHER
(WHAT IT MEANS...WHY IT MATTERS)

There is an old an oft-repeated adage that says, "The family that <u>prays</u> together, <u>stays</u> together." In a world where many families are being ripped apart by enormous pressures both from within and from outside, we might all do well to understand and heed this advice.

The first thing we need to do, however, is to <u>understand</u> what it says. It may easily be interpreted simplistically if one takes it in in a superficial way, but I'm inclined to look a bit deeper. A greater richness may be lurking just below the surface of what seems like only a simple statement of truth.

The word "pray" means "to ask very earnestly." It means to express a desire for something seriously and intensely. It represents a zealous and sincere request for something that is wanted or needed. Obviously, it makes sense to direct this kind of energy to a source that is capable of fulfilling the prayer. This is why we most often think of prayer in relation to deity or divinity of some kind. And for the vast majority of us, that deity is a monotheistic God who is Omniscient, Omnipotent, Omnipresent and All-Inclusive. But we might also direct a prayer (in a generic sense) to any power greater than us, which we see as in a position to meet our expressed needs.

Regardless of how we pray, we ought to know, I think, that prayer is very powerful. When we pray...when we focus the energy of our desires toward what we see as the source of our good... we get answers to our prayers. We <u>get</u> answers if we are <u>open</u> to them, have <u>faith</u> that they will come, and when we don't have rigid, pre-conceived notions about what the answers should <u>be.</u>

There is another old saying that warns us to "be careful what [we] ask for because [we] just might get it." Sometimes what we perceive as our highest good may, in fact, be very detrimental to us if we should actually have it. It helps to ask for things that we are really ready for. That's one reason why it helps to pray together. But if we are to pray together—especially as families—don't you think we should discuss what to pray for?

A teenage son might pray for a new motorcycle; his dad may covet a new position with his company. The mother may earnestly desire a new baby to love while little sister may crave a room of her own that she doesn't have to share with the daughter who is the middle child. The second born child may want only to be noticed and appreciated more by the members of her family.

But what happens if their prayers proceed and are answered independently? The new motorcycle may bring with it a serious injury. The new job may take too much of Dad's time away from his family. A new baby may make Dad's increased salary a break-even proposition especially if a new house must be bought to accommodate the baby and the prayer of the youngest daughter. At the same time, the eldest daughter's prayer may be put on hold, or she may get the notice and appreciation she wants but for reasons she might never have anticipated. It might be for helping the family cope with serious health-related ramifications presented by her big brother's motorcycle mishap.

Of course, this whole scenario might turn out in a completely different way, but that could not be truer than when the family chooses to coordinate their desires…and their prayers. If all of them are praying for the same thing; if they are pursuing a common vision; maybe their combined prayer energies will have a better chance of bringing a fruitful outcome for all of them.

Perhaps the family can create a reality where they move to a new (and larger) home, with a new family member, and a renewed commitment to a quality family experience for all of them. At the same time, the garage of the new house might have enough space for exciting new transportation for the son that has four wheels rather than two. And Dad's career goals might be met without sacrificing his family.

The family that prays together, stays together. What are the chances that this saying has a ring that sounds a little more resonant to you now?

FAITH
(ETHEREAL EVIDENCE)

In the Bible, the first verse of the eleventh chapter of the Book of Hebrews says, *"Now faith is the substance of things hoped for, the evidence of things not seen."* I have always loved those words. They do an excellent job of concisely expressing the essence of what faith is.

The power of faith, however, is probably one of the most misunderstood, maligned and underused of the many powers that are available to us. There is an on-going debate, for example, about whether or not faith is anything more than a comfort in the absence of hard evidence and a mere coincidence when the evidence actually matches the expectation.

But for those who seem to best exercise the power of faith in their lives, the comfort comes from a knowing rather than anticipation, and from the self-fulfillment of the prophetic nature of faith rather than coincidental occurrences.

Those who teach methods of visualization often instruct us to behave as if we are already in possession of that which we visualize. Those who correctly exercise the power of faith do the same thing. In many ways, the substance of what is envisioned is enjoyed before the reality of it is ever manifested in tangible form. True faith is the substance of what is hoped for—not an abstract idea about it. That distinction makes an enormous difference in whether faith is "real" or not and what grows out of it.

Those who are to one degree or another gifted with certain extra-sensory perceptions are able to accurately predict events that have not yet occurred because they can see or sense something that those who are more normally gifted cannot. In some way, they already have evidence of a future occurrence before others can discover the same or similar evidence. But, apparently, those who have unwavering faith can often do the very same thing. Faith is the evidence of things not seen.

It is difficult to convince the uninitiated of the validity of faith as a precursor of things to come, but anyone who ever demonstrates the fruits of immutable faith in their lives becomes initiated. All it takes is for the substance and evidence of something anticipated becoming real a few times, and we start to believe. On the other hand, all it takes to start disbelieving is for something we foresee to apparently not come to pass. How fickle we can be!

When the seeds of doubt start to grow, we must ask ourselves if we have been patient enough. We must ask ourselves if our vision is clear. We must determine whether or not we believe in the vision so much that we are already behaving "as if" we were experiencing the actuality. We must know whether or not the evidence is present before the thing is seen.

Faith is like any other tool: we must know what it is and how to use it before it will do us any good. The problem for most of us is that we are not sure about either. Yet if we can somehow grasp the truth behind the words as expressed in this particular scriptural reference, I think we'll have it made. I believe we can do it…and to a greater degree than we ever have before. All we need is a little faith.

AGITATIONS: OF WATER AND SPIRIT
(TRADING WHITEWATER RAPIDS FOR A GLASSY SEA)

Water seeks its own level; and when it finds it, it's still. Unless it's agitated by precipitation, the force of wind, the call of gravity, falling objects, or active life forms such as busy beavers, various fishes, or kids swimming at a church picnic, its surface remains completely unrippled.

The story is much different, however, when water is in the process of finding its level. Rain may fall on top of a hill or mountain where it begins to collect in small rivulets that eventually become creeks and streams, which grow ever larger. Heeding the call of gravity, these currents begin a headlong dash to the nearest significant level ground.

Along the way, rough terrain may turn the currents into whitewater rapids. Cliffs and steep, rocky hills may change them into roaring waterfalls. Great convergences of them may become mighty rivers. Other obstacles or challenges may make for eddies, whirlpools, or currents below the surface that are even more pronounced than what is apparent as we view the more obvious activity.

Eventually, however, the water will reach a point where it is no longer compelled to move. Perhaps it reaches the sea and is swallowed by its vastness. Maybe it reaches a lake or pond. By chance it may collect in puddles on a city street, or create a lake in the nearest suitable valley. In any case, it will no doubt find a place to come to rest; and when it does, only the most powerful and determined forces can make it move again.

If enough water collects in one place, there might be any number of forces that could disturb its exterior. But there is a depth at which those disturbances might just as well not exist, because they would be of no consequence. If we were some aquatic creatures who could, by means of some special discerning power always find such a level in such a body of water, any agitations we might perceive or experience on or near the surface would be merely temporary. The peace of the depths would ultimately be ours.

Likewise, our spirit seeks its own level; and when it finds it, it's still. Unless it is agitated by precipitous troubles, the force of "evil," the call of survival, falling from grace, or active life forms such as bosses, various friends and acquaintances, enemies, or kids swimming at a church picnic, it, too, remains completely unrippled.

This story, too, is much different when we are in the process of finding our level. We may fall from the top of a mountain of success where bits and pieces of our shattered psyches may begin to collect in little rivulets that eventually become creeks and streams growing ever larger. Heeding the call of survival, these currents begin a headlong dash to the nearest significant level ground.

Along the way, our difficulties may bounce us with relentless urgency through whitewater rapids, over awesome, roaring waterfalls, and with compulsive force along the paths of mighty rivers of overwhelming experience. Other circumstances or challenges may create psychological eddies, whirlpools, or currents below the surface that are even more pronounced than what is apparent as we interact based on the facades we put up as our official personas.

Eventually, however, we will reach a point where we are no longer compelled to move. For some of us, that may not come until we have reached the end of our days. For even in sleep, some of us wrestle in dreams and nightmares the demons we cannot vanquish in the waking hours.

If we could only learn to find the depths of soul that are available to each of us, we could live very much like the hypothetical marine creature we considered a moment ago—always at peace even as life's storms rage all around us. Instead, we always rush, rush, rush through our experience and take too little time to gather ourselves in the calm pool of inner peace. Any one of us can access this inner sanctum if we simply take the time and establish the proper focus.

For all people, there exists a peaceful pool of consciousness as big as the sea and even more universal. Nevertheless, there seems to be nothing more difficult for us to do to find it than to mimic Reinhold Niebuhr and pray, "Grant me the serenity to accept the things I cannot change, the courage to change the things I can, and the wisdom to know the difference." And lest we think that the resulting inner peace is an idle sort, we might want to consider this anonymous corollary to Niebuhr's famous prayer: "If I'm not at home accepting the things I cannot change, I'm out changing the things I cannot accept."

The place of peace is also a place of renewal that gives us strength for the inevitable agitations that come. Find it, and you find a greater you.

DOUBT OR FAITH
(CHOOSING HOW TO PROCEED WHEN DOUBT SEEKS TO DOMINATE)

An e-mail pen pal sent me a little poem once that caught my attention. I have since tacked it onto the wall over my workstation. She did not post a source for the verse, so I have no idea where it originated. But this is what it says:

> Doubt sees the obstacles;
> Faith sees the way.
> Doubt sees the darkest night;
> Faith sees the day.
> Doubt dreads to take a step;
> Faith soars on high.
> Doubt questions, "Who believes?"
> Faith answers, "I!"

Frankly, I'm glad this rhyme came into my life when it did. One cannot get too many reminders about the value of faith. You have to believe in something, or you can't even get through your days. But in the same way most of us believe we'll sleep tonight and awaken in the morning, we ought to also believe in some of those aims and goals that we are inclined to believe are improbable or impossible.

I'm always reminded of a quote from Richard Bach's ILLUSIONS... that says, "You are never given a wish without also being given the power to make it come true." In a lesson series called The Twelve Life Secrets, an achievement motivator named Robert Stuberg says almost exactly the same words. And in another, the more well-known Brian Tracy tells us that just the fact that we can imagine something probably means we have the ability to accomplish it.

Ultimately, you have to believe in <u>something</u>. You have to put your faith in <u>something</u>. Whether you trust God (as you understand God); or yourself; or the power of ideas; or the design of the Universe; or the abilities of others; or all of these; some foundation of faith must pull you forward through life, or you will simply die—actually…or figuratively. Either way, it's much less than you might experience if you <u>believe</u> in something.

Since my friend first shared her poem with me, her influence and others have helped me to make dozens of highly significant decisions based on a constantly renewed commitment to faith. As a result, I fully expect my life to be enhanced significantly by the decisions I make. Please realize that in order for me to even *say* this, it is an exercise in faith. And believe me, it's a little scary. When we are depending on the evidence of things we cannot see, we feel like we're on shaky ground. Yet if the ground of our faith is solid, then it is our shakiness that is a misperception.

That's why, for me, the sum total of my faith always begins with faith in an All-Encompassing God. That's a choice of ground for faith that has been proven again and again in my life—even in spite of my residual doubts. From there, faith is extended through faith in myself, faith in the power of ideas, and then the faith that is least dependable (and thus most frightening for me): faith in trusted others. But even here, the fear is often negligible because in my particular hierarchy of faith, God (as I understand God) comes first.

I often think and talk about faith and have shared with others who do the same. And no doubt, this subject has come up for you in many thoughts, readings, conversations, or sermons that have nothing at all to do with me. But there is one thing I want to be different about this occasion and that is a challenge I'll offer to you now.

Someone once said, "Do the thing you fear, and the death of fear is certain." What may also be true, in the words of Franklin Roosevelt, is that, "We have nothing to fear but fear itself." So the challenge for you is this: Within the next week, do something that's really important to you that you have been unnecessarily afraid to do. Just step out on the most firmly grounded faith you possess and don't let go until you have succeeded. Then, make a note of what happens as a result of your exercise in faith. If what I suspect is correct, you will have a great story to tell and a strengthening plank for the foundation of your faith.

SUBTLE ENERGIES
(ALTERNATE REALITIES WE MISS IN THE DAILY HUSTLE)

Have you ever felt the heartbeat of a tree? Have you ever heard the wind's voice speak to you? Have you ever lay on the ground and absorbed the vibrating pulse of Mother Earth?

Have you ever tried to get someone's attention just by looking at her or him and had the person suddenly turn toward you as if you had called out a name? Have you ever answered a ringing phone and been certain who the caller was before you ever heard a voice on the other end of the line? Have you ever uttered a phrase simultaneously with another person and used almost the exact same phrasing and rhythm?

If you have never done any of these things, then you are missing out on a whole world of subtle energies that are available to almost anyone who is willing to tune in. But you do have to tune in. These energies will never come looking for you; you must look for them in the places where they live.

We get so caught up in the hustle and bustle and noises and voices of everyday activities that we seldom slow down enough, or quiet ourselves enough to hear the thunder of silence, or the breezes of our own breaths, or the steady drumming of our own hearts. And yet, in the stillness of a night, or the awesome quiet of a peaceful dawn, all these sounds can be available to us—sounds that we would normally never hear.

There are also sights to behold: figures in the mist of a fog, a character in clouds, patterns in shadows, rainbows in a glass of water. You might notice a momentary strobe effect as a moving train breaks up the steady stream of light from headlamps of vehicles that wait with you on the opposite side of a railroad crossing at night.

Subtle energies are all around us all the time, an entire world of sensory input that is usually intangible. It's sort of like the hum of your car's engine which you can't hear because your stereo is too loud. It's like the ambulance siren that you don't notice until a dog starts howling next door. It's the tabby cat that almost blends into a beige carpet in the softening light of dusk. It's the answer to a prayer that you can only feel vibrating inside you when you focus completely on the listening.

We live in a world where our lives are a model of slavery. We are enslaved by our choices, our responsibilities, our busy-nesses, and our distractions. We are sometimes afraid, it seems, to allow ourselves the freedom of just being—not doing, but just being. Being alive, being quiet, being still, being aware, being fully awake, being open. When we allow ourselves to BE, we also allow the subtle energies to speak to us in their own ways. And the messages they bring are much different than the ones we usually get.

Messages from the subtle energies are the yin that we need to balance our yang. They are the messages of peace that we require as an antidote to all the messages of stress. They are balms for our pains. They are rainbows for our storms. They are the first crack of dawn after a pitch-black night.

They are essential.

SILENT ALARM

Silent Alarm
Resounding noiselessly
through my mind.
Something is wrong.
Hustling, bustling activ-
ity in my being
Screams, "EMERGENCY!"
Without a word being spoken.

Emotions are
Ushered quickly to places of safety
Where they
Can't interfere or lend
their vulnerability
To the threat.

Thoughts rush in
To meet the thing head on
And fight
With calm precision that which
Caused alarm.

Protective gear
Allows the thoughts to
dowse the fires
And shield
The psyche against the
winds that seek
Destruction.

At last,
The fires have raged for naught;
And the winds have breathed
Their last
Potentially destructive breath
In vain.

My Spirit
Wins, again, the newest battle
For control of Life's circumstances
And rests
In Equilibrium.

Was I gone long?

STRESS VERSUS REINHOLD NIEBUHR
(AND THE WINNER IS...YOU)

Although it would be a somewhat pointless endeavor, one could make a good case for stress being the root cause of epidemics of ailments from season to season, and not share a single idea of what to do about it.

Without making such a case, I would like to acknowledge the generative power of stress in various pathologies. I will not let it be said, however, that I didn't give you at least <u>one</u> idea for how to deal with whatever may be causing stress for <u>you</u>. In fact, what I'd <u>really</u> like to do is give you what I think is the world's best prescription for dealing with stress and the illnesses it can cause.

When I was a boy growing up in the bustling little Northeast Texas town of Texarkana, I often had the pleasure and challenge of working in a neighborhood grocery store that was owned and operated by my grandparents. It was a pleasure for more reasons than I shall relate to you here and now, and a <u>challenge</u> for one reason that I can sum up fairly easily: it was responsible for a sizable chunk of my education in the "School of Life."

I remember a day in particular when I learned an important lesson as I was working to stock the shelves and bins in the candy and cookie department. (You might guess that this was one of my favorite places to work, and you'd be right. Grandpa's one caveat to us was not to "eat up his profit.") When my task of the moment turned to displaying cartons of Jolly Rancher Kisses, my life would suddenly be changed forever.

For a while, the company that makes these popular little hard candies included a token in each carton—a 3" x 5" card imprinted with some motto, slogan or saying. Most of them were probably axioms that you would recognize. I remember them occasionally being words that one or more of my parents or grand-parents would repeat—often with fervor. At other times, they might as well have been encrypted in some sort of code for all the sense they made to me. Nevertheless, I would make sure they got to my grandmother (who saved them all.)

To my pre-adolescent intellect, one card had a message that seemed rather enigmatic when I first read it after removing it from the box. Actually, it wasn't so bad except for one word that I quickly determined was the root of my decoding dilemma. Everything else was as clear as a bell. At any rate, I had all but relegated it to the pile that contained the other cards I would take to my Grandma when I suddenly remembered the "context strategy" I had learned in school. You know…the one where if you understand all the words in a context that surrounds an unfamiliar word, you can sometimes deduce the meaning of the word that is unknown.

Well, I decided to give the message one more careful perusal. Suddenly, the meaning dawned on me like a swift and brilliant sunrise on a perfect, spring day. Once I understood the message, I vowed never to forget it because it immediately reduced my level of stress by at least half—if not considerably more.

So…what was it that leapt from the card to the depths of my young heart? The message is one that you have probably encountered more than once in your life—including within the preceding pages. In fact, for one reason or another, it's even possible that it means as much (or more) to you as it does to me. The words were a version of that proverbial Serenity Prayer: "Grant me the serenity to accept the things I cannot change, the courage to change the things I can, and the wisdom to know the difference."

It wasn't until years later that I discovered that there was one word missing on the card; that Reinhold Niebuhr was responsible for the original version; and that it is very significant to certain groups of people. The missing word was "God;" it is part of a larger prayer by Niebuhr (although it is sometimes attributed to St. Francis); and it is the adopted prayer of Alcoholics Anonymous and other 12-Step groups where it is referred to simply as "The Serenity Prayer."

As an eleven-year-old boy, I somehow connected with the spirit of this prayer in a way that indelibly instructed me to be calm enough to accept circumstances over which I ultimately have no control, to be brave and strong enough to work at changing things over which I can exert some influence, and to be wise enough to know the difference between the two.

What I have discovered over the years is that if you faithfully take these words as a prayer and direct them to the source of your good (whether you would say it's God, or not) you get exactly what you ask for. Stress has very little power over anyone who is smart enough to know the difference between things they can change, and things they cannot.

Stress is often directly related to the difference between the way things are and the way we would like them to be. When there is a difference, we either change it or accept it. It's that simple.

I'm no genius, but I figured that out when I was eleven. If I'm right to suspect you are a few years older than that, then you haven't a moment to lose. If you're still plagued by stress or resulting infirmities, why not revisit the comforting words of The Serenity Prayer.

WHY WORRY?
(CARE AND CONCERN VS. FRET AND FRUSTRATION)

Once, on a whim, I opened a dictionary and learned that the first definition listed for the word "worry" is not what you might think.

In my trusty <u>Webster's Collegiate</u>, the first definition actually says, "to harass or treat roughly with (or as with) continual biting or tearing with the teeth." You have to read down to the third definition to find the one that we commonly think of when we think of the word "worry." That one begins by saying "to cause to feel troubled or uneasy."

I thought perhaps the word "fret" would bring a different result for sure. Not so. The first definition there reads: "to eat away or gnaw," and the second is "to wear away by gnawing, rubbing, corroding etc." Now <u>that</u> got me to thinking.

Actually, I was thinking <u>before</u> I opened my handy lexicon. On at least two occasions, I had an opportunity to speak on the subject of stress and worry. One was in a workshop setting for junior high students. The other was with a beautiful group of men at a breakfast held in a church in my hometown. Both times, I tried to make a distinction between worry and concern and to advocate for the latter by far over the former. At this point, I'm even more convinced that there is a major difference.

Some of us worry when we have problems or challenges. But instead of systematically eating away or gnawing at our conundrums, we allow them to eat away or gnaw at us. We let them harass or treat us roughly rather than embrace them with focused attention and an eye open for both their solutions and their gifts. Challenges and problems do have both, you know... <u>solutions</u> <u>and</u> gifts.

There is a sense of frustration and helplessness that accompanies classic worry. Worry is an admission of either not having done our best to solve the concern, or not seeing ourselves as capable of marshaling the resources to address it effectively. In either case, it is not time for worry; it is time, instead, for careful concern and our best assertive efforts.

Now…here is the proverbial $64 question: If you make your best, possible, assertive and positive effort to deal with a challenging situation, why worry? You cannot do better than your best; so why let the problem continue to eat away at you when you've done the best you can do? And if you have not given your best effort, then your energy needs to be devoted to your next approach to solving the dilemma—not the most recent. Any energy you devote to "crying over spilled milk" (as they say) or kicking yourself for your laziness, error or apathy is counter-productive. So why worry?

Why should we fret when we find a situation in our lives that definitely needs to be improved? If we eat away or gnaw at the problem, with all our available energy funneled directly to the target until it is obliterated, that's great. But if we allow the problem to eat away or gnaw at us until we are slowly but surely obliterated, we have made a terrible mistake. We have given our problems power over us instead of exercising our inherent power over them.

Every problem has a solution. Every unraveling can be re-knitted. Every obstacle can be somehow traversed. Every challenging situation can be vanquished. Those of us who believe that will simply give our attention to the goal until it is reached, or until it apparently cannot be reached. And whether we ultimately succeed or fail, no amount of worry is going to improve the effort. Only our focused care and concern can do that. So… why worry?

PSYCHIC SAFETY
(FINDING A SAFE PLACE TO BE YOURSELF)

Somewhere along the way, a sad thing happens to most of us: we find it no longer safe to be ourselves. That's when we build our facades and start to behave in ways that are designed specifically to get the approval of persons whose acceptance we value.

For example, maybe it happens with our parents. Perhaps they really hoped their first child would be a boy, and a beautiful girl turned up instead. Dad plays with her a little too roughly and then is surprised at how fragile she is. A tiny little resentment pops up in him in those situations that he doesn't recognize, but which the girl's intuition doesn't allow to go unnoticed. She adjusts. She learns what makes the light come on in Dad's eyes and takes her first baby steps toward becoming an "approval junkie." At the same time, she may be denying an essential part of who she really is.

Mom may have a strange feeling, a little itch in the back of her mind whenever dad and daughter are happily bonding. the feeling may seem out of place along with the apparent joy she experiences. A lifetime may pass without her understanding that itch as jealousy; but the daughter may pick up the vibes and learn to choose different behaviors with dad when mom is present—just so mom can be more comfortable. In the process, another little piece of her persona is tossed aside.

In other instances, a son may not develop the athletic prowess his parents hoped for or counted on. A daughter may not exhibit the characteristics of an intellectual giant who can grow into the family law or medical practice. Younger siblings may be the family's black sheep or simply march to the beat of different drummers. Somehow, they learn that they are not as loved and appreciated when they are true to themselves as when they attempt to fit the expectations others have of them. Need for approval wins again.

Eventually friends and acquaintances and schoolyard idols compound the problem. Where family members may be subtle in exerting an influence that they may not even know they are exerting, peers are often very blunt about bestowing or withholding their approval. So, more adjustments are made.

When friends eventually become girlfriends, boyfriends, lovers, fiancés and spouses, another level of approval cultivation can be reached and often is. By then, people may have put aside so much of themselves that they have no idea how to define themselves apart from their relationships with others. A growing unhappiness may emerge while the real reason for it remains obscure or completely invisible.

Fortunately, for many of us, as we have opportunities to meet other people, we continue to occasionally take the risk of being ourselves, perhaps because it's natural or we feel like we have nothing to lose. Consequently, we are sometimes rewarded with people who accept us without adjustment and we discover that we also have something to gain: ourselves!

An acquaintance may be absolutely delighted with the way you laugh where others may have regarded your laughter as the sound of a chicken with hiccups. A new friend may appreciate your creative and artistic abilities and not need or want you to demonstrate any other genius.

One of your buddies may have one of the same habits that you have. Where others might be annoyed by it, this friend makes you feel immediately comfortable because he or she doesn't notice or comment about your habit because it is so naturally a part of him or her.

A new lover may love the way your hair falls wildly about your face when it's dried by the wind after you've been swimming. A new girlfriend may lovingly touch the scar that most other people avoid looking at. A new husband or wife may consider your extra forty pounds of girth as just more of you to love. Your mother- and father-in-law may give you more credit for being a valuable human being than your own parents do.

One of the greatest gifts we can give people is to love them just the way they are—to make it safe for them to be themselves with all of their idiosyncrasies. One of the greatest gifts we can give ourselves is to find a place where we can be ourselves and fully appreciate who we are in spite of the hoops we choose to jump through for others. One of the most flattering and joyful things we can say to another human being is, "You make it safe to be me."

For each of us, there ought to be at least one person that is as comfortable for us as an old shoe or a loyal pet. If we do no more than exist in their presence, they ask no more of us and we feel compelled to give no more than who we really are—the quintessential us.

LATE-IN', WAITIN', HURRYIN', AND WORRYIN'
(THE BANES OF A HARRIED LIFE)

Often when we are moving purposely through the jam-packed itineraries of our harried lives, we can wind up doing what I call "Late-in', Waitin', Hurryin' and Worryin'. Some of this is unavoidable. Some of it is counter-productive. All of it is manageable. Perhaps in the spirit of a certain cleric from Assisi, we can learn to accept the parts we can't change, to change the things we can, and to be smart enough to figure out which is which.

"Late-in'" is what we're doing when we sound like the rabbit from Alice In Wonderland: "I'm late! I'm late...for a very important date! No time to say hello! Good-bye! I'm late, I'm late, I'm late!"

Sometimes we're late because we have desisted in our opportune endeavors to address the on-going existential exigencies that would otherwise necessitate our most expeditious exertions. In other words...we've been "goofing off," and have found ourselves with too little time to accomplish too much.

Procrastination is one of the ubiquitous evils from Pandora's box that is no doubt responsible for a multitude of others. If I figure out how we can remove that curse from our experience, I'll let you know. Meanwhile, if you beat me to it, I'll be one who will gladly help you make your first million as the author of a "How To" book on the subject.

Sometimes we're late from trying to do too much. There are still far too many of us that don't realize that sometimes we have to say no to our own wishes and those of others as a matter of self-preservation. We all get the same 24 hours in a day and a certain (but limited) amount of energy that we can apply to a "do-list" that never stops expanding. "Just Say No" means a lot more than keep away from drugs.

Occasionally, we are late from legitimate delays, from scheduling events too tightly, or not allowing enough leeway for unexpected contingencies. Then whatever causes our progress to lag disturbingly behind our intentions and/or someone's expectations will probably be complicated sometimes by "waitin'."

"Waitin'" is what we often invariably end up doing when we're late or hurrying. I mean, how often do you make every green light when you've got only twelve minutes to make a trip by car that would take ten minutes on the best day? If your experience is like mine, this will be when you deal with rush-hour traffic, a driving rainstorm, an unexpected road crew, a traffic accident, a slow-moving train, or a vigilant traffic cop.

Then there's "hurryin'" which is what we engage in when we're hoping we can make up for lost time. Our blood pressure rises. We get a death grip on the steering wheel. We make obscene gestures and utter expletives to innocent fellow travelers. We do O. J. Simpson styled sprints through crowded airport concourses carrying too much baggage. And if we're not careful, we gain a new but unwanted appreciation for the old adage, "Haste makes waste."

Often, hurryin' may not be so necessary. It may be if your boss will fire you for being five minutes late. It may not be if it only means missing out on your favorite pew at church.

To worsen matters, we add to our stress by "worryin'." That's when we paint vivid "worst case" scenarios in our minds about all the things that will go wrong if and when we arrive at our appointed rendezvous a little (or a lot) too late. The things we imagine as we scurry along would make feature-length Hollywood movies if we could play them out in real time. But more often, they fade to a mere momentary annoyance—like nightmares vanishing in the light of day.

Forget worryin'. It won't help, and it usually takes your mind off what you're doing to get there. Have you ever found yourself worrying about what's next when you're stopped in traffic and as a result you miss a golden opportunity to switch lanes, or to make a turn to another route where you can continue?

Let's face it, even our best plans will be frustrated from time to time; so when they are, make the best of it! Read part of a magazine article, re-read your files, file your nails, or make up a song while you're waiting for that "midnight train to Georgia." Re-think what you're currently doing or what you plan to do. Often, you'll discover a way to improve your current plan on the fly.

Be more assertive (but not reckless) in your effort to arrive alive and on time. Use your old football skills to run through a crowd untouched by would-be "tacklers." Alter your route and go around or under the train by way of an underpass. And pay strict attention to all occasions when your hurrying proves to have been unnecessary. Sometimes being detained is a message or a blessing.

Most of all, spend all your energy on your best effort to meet expectations and realize that you can't do better than your best. That should banish the last of the demons of "Late-in', Waitin', Hurryin' and Worryin'.

WHEN THE WEIGHT GETS LIFTED
(STRENGTH AND FREEDOM AFTER LIFE HAS BEEN HEAVY)

Sometimes life can really get heavy. It may feel as if the weight of the world is on your shoulders. At times like these, you may need to borrow admonitions from the world of weightlifting and say to yourself, "Tough it out! No pain; no gain!" or "You can do it!"

Sometimes when our life experience gets really heavy, we can (and perhaps we should) use it to strengthen ourselves. If we never had difficulties in life, we wouldn't have much to strengthen our characters, our constitution, our resolve, our life skills, or our mental fortitude.

In the gym, weight-lifters who are interested in muscle toning, flexibility and endurance lift relatively light weights and go for increased repetitions. Such a routine is usually geared towards maintaining a physique that has already been developed. But people who want to develop size and strength use heavier weights and fewer repetitions.

When we encounter troubles in our lives that are easily manageable, we are able to maintain a lifestyle that we have already attained with relatively little effort. It's pretty much business as usual with perhaps a temporary setback or a minor emergency or two to deal with along the way.

When we encounter major difficulties in life and struggle with them, we gain strength and, in a sense, make ourselves bigger people who have a greater capacity for dealing with problems we may meet in the future. And for each of the major difficulties we vanquish, we find that there are more of life's challenges that, by comparison, seem smaller than they used to. When we can see that, our lives become much easier to manage.

Occasionally, the weight we take on in the gym or in life may be more than we can bear. When that happens, it's good to have a spotter. Spotters are people who have some strength of their own and who are not currently struggling with their own weighty issues. For your sake, though, the most important requirement is that they be nearby to lend a hand if you get in trouble with the weight you're trying to handle.

In the gym, spotters may have to exert themselves very little in order to help you get your weights "over the hump" represented by your point of weakness or exhaustion. In life, it may be no different. But in both cases, it could be disastrous if they're not there to help you through the tough times that would be too great for you to face alone.

Being able to increase your prowess at dealing with weighty concerns does wonders for your confidence in either arena—in the gym. or in life. The more you are able to take on, the more you know you are capable of taking on. Then when life deals you some of those unpleasant surprises that it's known for, you feel much more prepared and competent. You might even become a spotter for someone else.

Sometimes the best thing we can do as spotters when we are helping someone else is to know when not to help. Sometimes we can use our intuition and get a sense for when a word of encouragement can help our partner or friend push past the point where they feel like they can't go on. Sometimes if we just say, "Go ahead; you can do it!" or "Tough it out!" they get a sense for our belief in them and are secure in knowing that we really are there for them if they get overwhelmed. That can give them the courage to reach deep inside themselves for that extra little bit that allows them to be successful.

Of course, dealing with weights of any kind is a lot easier when you know you can take it or leave it. It's different when you know you can walk away at any time or that there's an end to the routine somewhere that will allow you to move on. But it's a different circumstance when you can't escape the weight, when it becomes a burden that you could wind up having to bear alone most of the time.

Handling this kind of weight alone makes you tired. It saps your energy. It ages you. It etches lines on your face. It robs you of your joy. It will ultimately destroy you unless you can somehow reduce or eliminate its pressure.

In this case, you either recruit so much help for dealing with it that its heaviness becomes negligible; you pass it on to someone who can handle it better than you; you let go of it; or you destroy it.

Whichever path you take will change everything if you wind up free of the weight. There will be a new light in your eyes, a new spring in your step, a new lilt in your voice, a new hope in your heart.

When life gets heavy, you have a choice to either get stronger or claim your freedom. If you can do either or both without harming yourself or someone else, you owe it to yourself to do so. So what are you waiting for? "Tough it out!"

BURNING BOTH ENDS OF THE CANDLE
(WHEN YOU NEED MORE OF YOUR OWN LIGHT)

I have a confession to make: I sometimes burn the candle that is me at both ends. Oh, I'm always <u>careful</u> about it. But sometimes, I just can't figure out what else to do.

I suppose I would never do it if I were lazy. If I wasn't highly motivated to make things happen, I could just blow off some of the things I do… maybe even a <u>lot</u> of the things I do. I certainly wouldn't be alone. There are lots of lazy people in the world. I just prefer to be one of the industrious ones. There are things <u>I</u> want to <u>do!</u>

I sometimes think it would be easier if my priorities were just a little bit clearer. Of course, they're <u>fairly</u> clear already. I <u>work</u> at that <u>regularly</u>. I think I'm getting things pretty much in the right order and doing okay at keeping first things, first. But what I have trouble with is the fact that so many things insist on crowding themselves into the <u>first</u> slot on the list. It seems like I often have a half dozen or so responsibilities, needs or desires that all shout the same chant: "We're number one! We're number one!"

Heck, they can't <u>all</u> be number one! I'm not that good at juggling.

Maybe it would be easier if I just learned to say "no" more often. Then again, I'm not exactly a dyed-in-the-wool "<u>yes</u>" man. I say "no" fairly often to the things and the people that require my time and energy. And I don't have a problem with the things I say "no" to. It's just that the things I say "yes" to seem to keep piling up now and then.

I used to think it would be easier if I just said, "To heck with it!" and then just "let sleeping dogs lie" as they say. Sooner or later, though, the dogs start barking; or one or more of them sneak up and take painful nips out of me when I least expect it. Occasionally, it seems like there are suddenly more of them awake than there were when I counted them as they slept.

Finally, I decided that I could get more bang for my buck if I changed my paradigm for how I viewed my ability to meet challenges. I decided to defy conventional wisdom. I decided to tempt fate a bit. I decided to push the envelope. I decided to light the other end of my candle. There was more of me that I could put to use.

So far, I've been lucky. I've seen people who started out toying with burning their candle at both ends and before they knew it, the flames were beginning to meet in the middle and suddenly their light was snuffed out (or nearly so.)

Then again, maybe I've just been more careful, or shrewder, or more cautious, or more creative, or more farsighted, or more reflexive...or more evolved. In fact, I might be "preaching to the choir" as the saying goes. Maybe you, too, have discovered that bold measures are required for an ever more challenging and demanding world.

We are required, these days to do more with less—less time, less money, less sleep, less support, less appreciation, and sometimes even less self-satisfaction. But we are doing it!

We learn to juggle progress on two or more important projects until they are completed. We delegate, and team, and ask favors to extend our reach. In the economic arena, we budget tighter, bargain more, and spend less . Some of us are even rediscovering barter.

Maybe you, too, are finding that a few shortened nights every now and then can make a substantial difference if you wisely use the time that's gained. If we stay up late and get up early and catch up on our rest when we can; we may quickly discover that our ends are more easily reached (or at least more clearly in sight) and that moments of leisure return.

But we must be ever vigilant. Otherwise, there are deceptive little gremlins that exist primarily to make us believe that we're invincible, that more is better, that there are no <u>practical</u> limits. Don't be deceived.

You may be a super man or a wonderful woman, but you are not Superman or Wonder Woman. Experiment with pushing your personal envelope of capability; today's world asks for that. But if you begin to hear ripping and tearing sounds, don't mistake them for the sounds of success. It may be your envelope telling you you've gone far enough.

CARRY ON
(OR BECOME CARRION)

I have a friend who used to present a workshop that he called "Grow or Die." Put another way, I guess the idea is that we either carry on...or become carrion.

Naturally, in this context, to "carry on" means to "manage or conduct" (as in business or affairs) or to "continue without stopping." Assuming that we are already managing our lives pretty well, then we simply need to continue without stopping...to persevere. Of course, if we feel more like our lives are managing us, then perhaps we need to carry out instead. In this case, carrying out a better plan for living would be the ticket. Otherwise, we may become carrion.

My unabridged dictionary's first definition for carrion is "dead and putrefying flesh."…. Yuck! The very thought of that is almost as vile as the reality. But what's true is that left to the ways of nature, this is what our bodies become when we set them aside at death. And yet the more figurative understanding is what we are really after.

If life is at times like traveling through a barren land, a desert; as long as we keep moving, we have a chance to get through to a more hospitable place. But if we stop for too long, or give up, the vultures start circling and will eventually swoop down to see if they can feed off what is left of us. Carry on or become carrion.

The 17th Century English poet, Robert Herrick, puts it this way: "If well thou hast begun, go on foreright; it is the end that crowns us, not the fight." It is the end that crowns us—what we can accomplish. And what we can accomplish depends almost solely on what we carry out...and whether we carry on.

While captive in a waiting room once, I watched a couple of those ubiquitous daytime talk shows. They were the kind that tends to degenerate into shouting matches with lots of expletives deleted by the sound of the editor's handy "beeper." The back-to-back shows were both about wild teenagers who—despite their claims of loving themselves and others—were dangerously engaged in varying stages of promiscuous sex and violence and other acting out behaviors. No doubt, at <u>some</u> point in their young lives they had been on a path toward being successfully socialized into mainstream society; but they stopped carrying on (as in perseverance) and <u>started</u> carrying on (as in misbehaving).

Instead of carrying on with plans like the ones that suffice to bring fulfillment for most people, these troubled teens carry on with various self-destructive and anti-social agendas. Maybe they can't see it now, or perhaps they are ignoring it; but the vultures are already circling. The scavengers know that if they have not already feasted on what's left of the human that used to be alive inside those young bodies, it's just a matter of time before they will. Somewhere along the way, those kids stopped growing and started dying. And the saddest part is that in many ways, they haven't even lived yet.

Let's remember, though, that they have to learn vitality from someone. When they look to you, make sure that there are no buzzards circling around your head. Carry on!

WHO ARE WE?

Out there
As opposed to: IN.   HERE.,
There's something
That is directly responsible
For ME—
Meaning all that I am;
But It's also IN HERE.
I am It   and
It is me.   Yet
It is greater
Than I.
I know
Because It was here
Long before I was.

Want to know
How Great It Is?
It is you...
And It is Everything Else.
Does that answer your
Question?
Yet, I am It   and
It is me   and
It is you.   So
You are me   and
We're no less   than
All It Is;   So
Maybe we   should
Learn just WHO we are!

WHY WE CAN ALL BE SUCCESSFUL
(AND WHY MANY OF US WON'T)

I've been toying with an assertion about the relationship between the average human, and success as most of us understand it. And if not success as most of us understand it, at least success as H. G. Wells is said to have defined it. This well-known British author has said that the measure of success is the difference between what we might have been and what we have actually accomplished in life.

At any rate, my assertion is that there are universally valid reasons why all humans can be successful (at least by the Wellsian definition) and also a good handful of reasons why many of us will not.

In a nutshell, I believe that we can all be successful because: (1) we all have innate, diverse and viable abilities; (2) we are all infinitely capable of learning; (3) we all have practically limitless opportunities to develop our abilities into talents and skills; and (4) the total world we live in gives us access to unlimited power, unlimited total resources, unlimited needs to be filled, and infinite material and ethereal universes to explore.

On top of all that: (1) we have the power of dreams and visions which become precursors to realities we can manifest; (2) we can experience quantum leaps in our abilities from the simple act of cooperation; and (3) we're fortunate to occupy a beautiful, life-sustaining planet.

Barring those of us with the most severely debilitating disease, dysfunction, or disability, even the weakest among us have innate, diverse and viable abilities and are infinitely capable of learning. Some of us have more innate abilities than others and some of us are quicker studies than others;

but opportunity and hard, enthusiastic work tend to be great equalizers especially when coupled with cooperation. As for the practically limitless opportunities to develop our abilities into talents and skills, every day we live brings them to us (or us to them.) Only losing our lives takes away these opportunities.

Power, resources, needs and unexplored areas are limitless in our Universe. That's as easy to imagine as the infinity of existence, itself; and the latter has been scientifically <u>proven</u>. Add to that the proven dynamics of physical things emerging from those which first exist only in mind, heart and spirit, and limitations to our success become mere figments of our imaginations.

Oh, it is definitely possible for all of us to be successful...to realize much more of our innate potentials. But, in another nutshell, I can tell you why many of us will <u>not</u> be successful. It is because: (1) various circumstances will keep our innate, diverse and viable abilities hidden from our view; (2) we will either be too frightened, too lazy, or too oppressed to explore our infinite learning capability; (3) we will miss or squander far too many of our practically limitless opportunities to develop our abilities into talents and skills; and (4) those of us who can, will selfishly limit others' access to the unlimited power, resources, and perception of needs that need to be filled.

This is not a hopeless view; but it is one that suggests a prescription for making things different. Each of us must explore innate abilities at all costs, let nothing prevent learning, take advantage of all opportunities for growth, and know that the Universe is pleased to provide us with what we need for success. This is a tall order, for sure; but it is also one that can be filled.

WATERMELON SEEDS
(A LESSON ON POTENTIAL)

Perhaps you are one of many people who occasionally enjoy an ice-cold slice of watermelon. If not, you can still probably relate to an experience a watermelon eater has probably had a number of times: getting seeds in your mouth.

Unless you meticulously extract every visible seed (and probe for all the invisible ones), invariably you will find one of the hundreds of white, brown, or black seeds vying for the trip down your esophagus. And if you're like most people, you spit them out.

But, of course, every time you spit out a seed, you are also probably banishing it to a permanent exile among countless other items of garbage… and its potential is lost. It's not such a great loss in the overall scheme of things; many other seeds do get the opportunity to become one of the huge fruits and to give birth to hundreds more seeds that are the spittin' image of themselves. (Go ahead; enjoy the pun.)

But in the life of each single seed, the loss is enormous! Its potential will probably never be realized. And what a tremendous potential it is! There have been some state-fair, record-breaking melons big enough to be the entire payload of a small pick-up truck. Imagine the number of seeds that would be in that baby! And with heredity being what it is, other record-breakers being born in that lineage are likely.

What's really miraculous is that such a gigantic fruit could emerge from a little teardrop shaped package that is much less than a sixteenth of an inch thick and barely a quarter of an inch long. Yet what is more awesome is that seeds much smaller can create even larger fruits than the watermelon.

Consider for a moment how astounding it is to witness the fruits represented in the life of the average human being. We emerge from tiny seeds that are literally microscopic in size. If the watermelon amazes you, the fruit-bearing capabilities of the human seed should <u>regularly</u> leave you in jaw-dropping awe.

We can be pretty casual about watermelon seeds we lose; and to a degree, I suppose we can be less than disturbed by losing a few of the microscopic <u>human</u> seeds.

It's true that a watermelon farmer might not lose any sleep if a few watermelons in the field rot, get eaten by vermin, or fail to mature into edible fruit. There will be many other melons, no doubt, that will more than make up for the loss. But here is where the human experience, by comparison, starts to veer sharply onto a far different course.

Ours is a society where more and more people are in danger of never achieving more than a mere fraction of what is possible for them—even with a fertile environment and proper care and cultivation (which many do not have). Sadly, we cannot be the least bit cavalier about this loss. The unrealized possibilities of <u>any</u> human are FAR more tragic than one less watermelon at the fruit stand.

If you can picture in your mind a tiny watermelon seed in one hand and a hundred-pound watermelon in the other, you also have a pretty good picture of the difference between what many people <u>realize</u> about themselves in a lifetime and what they <u>might</u> realize under far more empowering circumstances.

When you consider this scenario, tears may not well up in your eyes; but if your <u>heart</u> sheds a tear for this tragedy, let this tiny tear give birth to a commitment to cultivate the life of at least one human (for whom you are not duty-bound to take responsibility.) If we each commit to caring for others until their roots are strong, and their leaves and flowers are independently and powerfully yearning for more of the limitless possibilities of the unique human experience; we will be farmers in a way that the watermelon grower would have to envy.

THE INN IS NOT HOME
(WHAT DOES BEING "COMFORTABLE" REALLY MEAN?)

Saint Augustine is quoted as saying, "...[T]he man journeying to his own country must not mistake the inn for his home." At first blush, one might read or hear that statement and say, with a healthy dose of righteous indignation, "Well, of course not! How could anyone do that?"

Just the same, we do often get a little too comfortable in places that are not "home" for us. We at least consider staying in locales that are not suited for who we are or what we need. We may, in fact, set up camp and stake a claim. In both a literal and a figurative sense, this is much too likely for each of us.

We can start with homes, themselves, and consider that some of us pay a lot more to rent a property that belongs to someone else than we would to purchase a more modest abode that we might eventually call our own. Sometimes that makes sense; but there are also times when we allow ourselves to get trapped into that choice as if there weren't another. We may be comfortable, indeed; but is that really home?

We can also wind up either getting attached to a manageable but dead-end job, or settling into a career where the sky is the limit but the personal cost to us (and perhaps to our families) is enormous. We may be enjoying a certain security, or status, or income level, or material possessions; but considering that we often spend a good third of our adult lives in gainful employment, shouldn't we be certain that we are at home with what we choose as a vocation?

The darkness of ignorance, prejudice, negativity, or low self-esteem can also get very comfortable. Along the road to finding ourselves, these places to hang our hats and lay our heads are easy to find and just as easy to adopt as the places we're supposed to be. We often come to them on the recommendation of someone who has already chosen to live there because they have mistaken this wayfarer's rest stop for a permanent home.

Home, in this case, is really enlightenment, openness and tolerance, and a positive and productive sense of self, relationship, and purpose. That's where we ought to be.

Behaviors, too, become very comfortable and sustaining and we hasten to call many of them home when, in fact, we're stuck in an inn instead. For those of us who do this (and most of us do) it can easily be among our worst errors.

We often choose behaviors early in life that are legitimately self-protecting in some way and then we wind up keeping them forever even though they may have outlived their usefulness by years. When this happens, the behaviors—at least—become a part of the unnecessary baggage we carry around and at worst become self-defeating or even self-destructive. We must be careful not to be too at-home with some of our behaviors.

For some of us, even our families are more like the inn than home. By accident of birth (so to speak) we are all born into our families of origin; and though we are obviously prepared for them, they are not necessarily prepared for us.

If our first families are not prepared to nurture us in ways that are necessary and appropriate for our growth and development and self-actualization, we would do well to find where home really is. It may be found with other family members or in quiet talks with a next-door neighbor. It may be with a minister or priest or counselor. It may be with a teacher or best friend or buddies in the army. Then again, it may not be found until we have an opportunity to create our own home. Whatever the case, we would do well to discover what home needs to be in order for us to live there.

Friendships, too, can be temporary stopping places rather than destinations. True friends always have gifts for us when they come into our lives. They are mutually beneficial—in ways we can see, and often in ways we can't see. But when friendships are comfortable yet counterproductive, detrimental or destructive, we need to pack up our bags and keep moving toward friendships where we can really be at home, where we can be enlightened, empowered, supported, nurtured, loved and cared for. These would be the type of friendships where any person could be at home.

Finally, we might consider how too many of us make a home of the physical pleasures of life—drugs, sex, food, parties, laziness, and so on. I would be among the last to suggest that some of these simple pleasures are not occasionally appropriate. But I would be among the first to insist that none of them are worth indulging in for a lifetime. They are simply inns along the way that are meant for temporary comfort—if that. They are not meant to be dwelling places. They are not meant to be home.

BEING ON FIRE
(CONTROLLED IGNITION AND CONSUMPTION OF THE LIFE FORCE)

There is an analogy for the mystery of human life that seems to stay with me all the time. It has to do with what I like to call "The Great Creative Spark of the Universe" which is one of the ways I choose to think of God.

Actually, I think my concept of God the Spark is more like "The Great Creative <u>Bonfire</u> of the Universe." Ultimately, I suppose this semantic choice doesn't really matter. Great fires are notorious for having been started by a single spark. Just ask Smokey the Bear.

Thinking of God as a great bonfire, though, makes it easier to think of each of us as being sparks thrown off from the fire; and therein lies the analogy that intrigues me.

If you have ever sat and watched a roaring fire in a fireplace that features the snap, crackle and pop of certain volatile woods like hedge, for example; you have probably also witnessed a veritable fireworks display of flying sparks. No doubt, you or someone else may have also found it necessary to stamp <u>out</u> a persistent spark or two that threatened to ignite something else—like a sweater or a sofa or a carpet.

In the world of homes and fireplaces, smothering those persistent little bits of wood coal is a good idea. But for the enduring sparks of Life that each of <u>us</u> represent, the idea is to keep them burning as long, as hot, and as brightly as possible. We need to be <u>on fire</u> <u>all</u> our lives.

Maintaining and controlling life's ignition and consumption, however, is not an easy task. The trick is to fan the flame just enough to keep it at the vital temperature necessary for the goals of our lives without allowing it to extinguish...or burn us up too quickly. We have all seen people who are merely surviving with a life flame that is all but cold ash. We have probably also seen the folks who live far too exuberantly or recklessly and whose spark of life explodes into nothingness at a much too tender age. They are the ones who refuse to realize the delicacy of maintaining the fire over the long haul.

The other problem is to avoid all the dangers to continued burning. There are the waters of illness, disease, and injury. There are the stomping feet of mishap, and violence. There are the frantic brushing hands of expectation, responsibility, work, stress, and self-defeating life choices. There is also the unhappy fact that it's very difficult to find dependable guidance about how to optimally maintain the extraordinary flame of individuals who are (in some ways) as unique as each of their fingerprints.

Just the same, being on fire is what we must be—for as long as is humanly possible. And we must also burn for something that matters. Burning without purpose is the next worst thing to not burning at all, to mere existence. If we are born, we exist. Spiritual teachers say even if we are not born, we exist. That's the easy part. Fanning our flame properly is what's hard.

But as always, difficulty does not mean impossibility; nor does it mean that we should not arm ourselves with the best knowledge we can get about keeping ourselves aflame indefinitely. As long as it is true that I am a spark tossed off from The Great Bonfire, I plan to be operating the fire of my life at peak intensity. My hope is that we will all join together in this..."quest for fire."

BLOOD, SWEAT AND TEARS
(OR WOUNDEDNESS, WORK AND WOE)

No doubt, you are familiar with the expression "blood, sweat and tears." You might have even used it in conversation to demonstrate your (or someone's) level of commitment or investment in something. In fact, if you belong to the right generations or the right nostalgia group for popular music, you may immediately think of a classic rock and roll band which took that expression as a name. But have you ever stopped to consider what these three words really convey in the context of life?

Another way to express this triumvirate is with the words, "woundedness," "work," and "woe." Because these words are less idiomatic, they kind of make you take notice, don't they? They conjure up visions of the gray side of life experience which, of course, has its value, too.

The woundedness we experience in life is sometimes quite remarkable. I have met at least three people who have survived being struck by lightning. I know a number of people who have endured broken bones, experienced concussive blows to the head, survived stab or gunshot wounds, or managed to endure in spite of injurious automobile crashes. And my acquaintances with the walking wounded whose hurts are emotional or psychological are practically uncountable. For us to live lives devoid of damage to our personhood is impossible. To recognize the impact and value of our woundedness is imperative. Yet for many of us, it is also unlikely. We are more inclined to seek escape or forgetfulness rather than understanding when it comes to our wounds.

When we factor out the sweat we experience from heat alone, probably all other sweat is the result of work, of effort, of exertion. This, too is inescapable; and though many of us work less physically and more intellectually, the sweat of our labors is still possible for us figuratively—and also tangibly if you count the times that our sweat is the stress-related one we recognize as "a cold sweat." We can sometimes make choices where our work becomes inextricably tied to our joy, but even then, effort is unavoidable. We must pay for our experiences with sweat.

Likewise, our tears are sometimes tears of joy; but more often than not, even if they go uncried, they signal the presence of woe…of grief, worry, adversity, distress…of sorrow, anguish, pain, and remorse. These are certainly not pleasant things to dwell on; but like blood and sweat, we can count on the tears of woe being a part of our experience.

If we can just learn—and remember—to explore the meanings behind our life experiences, then perhaps the blood, sweat and tears we shed will be more fully recognized and take on ever greater significance. Our wounds will become our badges of courage; our work will become more attuned to our purpose—and thus more joyful. And our woes? I suspect they will begin to fade and dwindle in the light of our understanding.

DO IT TODAY
(PRIORITIZING THE MOST IMPORTANT THINGS)

I remember a time when my son and I both slept in on a particular day. We both needed it because we had been awake until almost 2 a.m. the night before. Mom was away. It was a boys' night up.

After a supper of homemade soup and a couple of slices of jalapeno cornbread, we ran an errand, watched a movie and then spent a couple of hours tweaking our computers and organizing our desks.

My son, Arri, had inherited a used computer. Together, we were improving our skills with the Windows operating system and learning to customize how it worked for us. At that point, I was teaching him a lot. At this point, he's beginning to teach me. He was only nine then, and he was already remarkably proficient.

But you know, it wasn't so much what we were doing together as it was the fact that we were doing it, doing it when we both wanted to, and loving every minute of it. It's always great when it effortlessly works out that way; but both then and now I'm paying more attention when effort IS required to set aside quality time with my son.

It seems that a conscientious and dedicated person can always find many things that need to be done. That's why I have often recited what amounts to sort of a mantra for me. It has been a kind of hymn of prayer that reminded me to "organize, prioritize and stay on task."

The thinking of Steven Covey has encouraged me to edit that motto a little. His <u>Seven Habits of Highly Effective People</u> puts those functions in a different order. For Dr. Covey, prioritizing comes before organizing. He underscores putting "first things first." Now this is not exactly news; but I am thankful for the reminder. If we are not careful, we can easily lose sight of our priorities if we don't focus on them first.

I have often spent time and energy considering the importance of unearthing a personal mission and encouraged others to do the same. Steven Covey, I have discovered, also emphasizes the value of this function. When you are clear about your mission, he says, your values and priorities are more easily recognized as the things that support your mission. Anything that doesn't may not be important, he adds.

He also warns us about the difference between what's urgent and what is important. He defines urgency as being characterized by those things that have the <u>appearance</u> of requiring immediate attention. He emphasizes appearance because ringing phones and doorbells, unopened mail, and the crises of others may be urgent but not necessarily important.

This insight has helped me to realize the error of attempting to get organized before my priorities are in line. What I think I've been discovering all along is that when my priorities are straight, the organizing seems a whole lot easier to accomplish.

An example is that for me, trying to clear my desk in my office seems a never-ending process. Most of the time, the fact that I have trouble getting it done drives me crazy. Lately, I have made my peace with the piles on the desk that are dwindling with agonizing slowness. I've recognized that I sometimes have more important things to do; things like hanging out with my son until the wee hours of the morning.

The author, Jim Kern, tells a poignant story about a man whose young son repeatedly invited his dad to help him build a fort in their back yard. Because other responsibilities were pressing him, the father delayed his acquiescence again and again until finally he promised his son that they would build the fort the next day.

The son was so excited that he could barely sit through classes at school the next day. Somehow, he managed and then dashed toward home as fast as he could. Unfortunately his excitement clouded his judgment and he dashed into a street without considering traffic. He never made it home.

Of the many things that it is important to do, none are more important than spending quality time with those we love. If you have been putting that off with someone you love, reorder your priorities, and spend that time today.

PRIORITIES AGAIN
(PUTTING INFINITE DO-LISTS INTO A FINITE ORDER)

I have a copy of a great story about an encounter Charles Schwab had with an efficiency expert when Schwab was president of Bethlehem Steel many years ago. The consultant's name was Ivy Lee, and Schwab simply asked him to suggest a way to improve the efficiency of his business.

As the story goes, Lee handed Schwab a blank sheet of paper and asked him to write down the six most important tasks he had to do the next day, and to number them in the order of their importance. He then added the following instructions:

> "The first thing in the morning, start working on number one until it is finished. Then tackle number two, and so on. Don't be concerned if you have only finished one or two by quitting time. You'll be working on the most important ones. The others can wait. If you couldn't finish them all by this method, you couldn't have done so by any other method; and without some system, you'd probably have failed to finish the most important.
>
> Do this every working day, and after you have convinced yourself of the value of this system, have your men try it. Try it as long as you wish, then send me a check for what you think it has been worth to you."

And now, the rest of the story, as Paul Harvey might say, is that apparently Schwab sent Lee a check for $25,000 a few weeks later. In an accompanying letter, Schwab exclaimed that Lee's lesson was the most profitable he had ever learned.

The first time I read this story, I was struck by the logic, and the elegant simplicity and power of what Lee shared. I had to shake my head and say, "Wow!" But another part of me wanted to smack myself on the head and go, "Duuuuuhhhhhhh!" Such a simple solution to the common everyday problem of having too much to do is the kind of thing we'd all expect to think of and employ with absolutely no prompting from the outside. But the fact is, this solution is not so obvious.

The key is Lee's suggestion that not only do we need a systematic and prioritized approach to the things we must do, but we also need to realize that if we can't finish all the things on our lists when we have them correctly prioritized, we can't do so by any other method either.

As much as I'd like to report otherwise, there are still only twenty-four hours in each day—and only a certain number of them can be focused on productive work. If we use that productive time by putting first things first (as Stephen Covey emphasizes in modern times) we will at least get the most important things done. If the rest can't wait (as Ivy Lee suggested), then it's time to ask for help. This, by the way, is another simple solution we sometimes overlook, so why don't we explore it next. My idea priorities are all used up for the moment.

NEEDING HELP

(ASKING FOR ASSISTANCE WITH DAUNTING CHALLENGES)

Many of us have probably felt (at one time or another) as if we have had too many things to do and not nearly enough time to do them. For some of us, this sense of being overwhelmed by our responsibilities is practically an everyday occurrence. This seems to be true even if we inhabit a highly developed world where we are surrounded by labor-saving technologies. Unfortunately, where we may enjoy devices and processes that save us time and effort on one hand, they sometimes create <u>more</u> work and responsibility for us on the <u>other</u> hand. Does this seem familiar?

Even for those of us who consciously and successfully work to <u>simplify</u> our lives, we may often find that a voracious horde of duties and obligations continues to descend upon us in swarming crescendos. The only escape seems to be into the life of a back-to-nature hermit. This is less than desirable for most of us at the same time that it is also probably beyond our current physical, psychological and sociological capabilities.

When we do wind up with far too much on our "To-Do" lists, learning to use our productive time more efficiently by prioritizing our goals and our work efforts according to their relative importance can help. But even then, we may be getting the <u>most</u> important things done while dropping the ball on lesser <u>priorities</u> that are no less <u>meaningful</u>. When meaningful goals are consistently being waylaid by even more significant goals, it's time to ask for help.

This, by the way, is one of the simplest of solutions to the predicament of having too much to do; but <u>choosing</u> the option of asking for help is not always as simple as the solution. Sometimes it's a matter of pride or vanity. Sometimes we feel that our responsibilities are tailor-made for us and not accessible to the understanding and skills of others. Sometimes we ask for help only to discover that those we ask feel as overwhelmed as we do. Sometimes the excuse we use for not asking for help is... whatever your particular reason happens to be. We all have our reasons for going solo with responsibilities, but none of them should keep us from getting help when we need it if we believe that what we choose to do with our lives is important. And for whom is that not true?

When you need help in meeting the daunting challenges you face, ASK! And if you don't get the help you need when you ask once, ask again... and again! It's the perfect time to remember the old adage, "If at first you don't succeed, try, try again." It's also a good time to remember, "There is more than one pebble on the beach." Where one doesn't meet your needs, another will.

Oh, and one more thing, when you ask for help, don't forget to consider two groups of potential helpers that are often very underemployed. In today's society, the energies and capabilities of young people are often vastly underused, and so are the skills and knowledge of the elderly. With young people, where juvenile delinquency is an easy result of idle minds and hands, your asking them for help could help prevent that. With older folks, the crime is that we are wasting a national treasure represented by the experience and skills of senior citizens by not asking for their assistance. We simply can't afford either.

Yes, there are still only twenty-four hours in each day—and only a certain number of them can be focused on productive work. But when more of us are focusing our time together and working toward common goals, more goals are reached. Learn to ask for help.

SLICE OF LIFE

Slice Of Life!
What a gorgeous metaphor!
Whether wafer thin
Or a slab,
The loaf
That is our life
Is sliced!

Grandma's smile!...
Sharing love that's
born of days
That are long since passed
But heart felt
And shared
With thoughtful warmth
Always.

Falling tears
From the eyes of some sad girl
Who could hardly drive
In her car...
I felt
Her nameless grief
And prayed.

Flying rice
And a frozen moment's time...
It's her wedding day,
And her folks
Are proud
Of what they've wrought
With love.

Blood and cries
From an accident with cars
In an ugly crash...
Sirens wail
To take
The victims to
Repair.

Flying kite
And a string that
is unmanned
Way up in the sky...
It will float
Away

And come to rest
Somewhere.

Great idea!
And it fell down from
the clouds
(So to speak, that is.)
Watch my life
Conform
To what I've thought
Just now!

Embers glow
In a fireplace laid to rest
After evening's warmth...
Scenes appear
To eyes
That look for them
In coals.

What a star!...
And she hugged me
when I gave
Her the cab I hailed.
I will feel
I know
Her when she's on
The screen.

Standing up
To applaud my humble gift,
People say to me
You are loved
For what
You've given now...
To us.

Running fast,
I have crossed my finish line
Now in record time!
I have chased
This goal
For two long years.
I win!

Empty space...
Soon to be a brand
new place...

It will never look
Just like this
Again.
With my own hands,
I'll build.

Firstborn child,
You are mine! I
watched you born!
I have never seen
Such a sight
As this...
And never will
Again!

Brand new car!
"Sexy" smell and smooth
response!...
So unlike the "bomb"
I just sold
To buy
This long-term debt.
What fun!?

Songs first heard
Stop me in my tracks to hear.
Music touches me.
I incline
My ear
To feel it soothe
My soul.

Overheard...
"See you later alligator!"
'Twas a child
To his Dad
As he
Was off to work
Again.

Slice Of Life!
What a gorgeous metaphor!
Whether wafer thin
Or a slab,
The loaf
That is our life
Is sliced!

REFOUNDING THE VILLAGE
(THE ADMONITION OF AN AFRICAN PROVERB)

An old African proverb says, "It takes a village to raise a child." The wisdom in that saying is as solid as a hunk of teakwood. If this wisdom is to be heeded, meeting the challenge of successfully raising children in this day and time may mean finding a way to successfully recreate villages of the type that can raise them. The latter challenge may be far the greater of the two.

A "village," in the sense that it is used in the proverb means a small, closely knit community; but so many of us live in big, impersonal cities and towns. The word "village" usually invokes pastoral images of the country, but the landscape is crowded and urban for many of us. People in a classic village usually know and care about each other and have a vested interest in each other's success because mutual survival usually depends on it. It seems different in today's world; but does it have to be? I think not.

There used to be a time when we could take villages for granted because that was how we lived. Nowadays, if we want to be part of a village we have to create one by making a close-knit community of our neighborhoods, our peer groups, or both. The good news is that it can definitely be done!

If we associate with or surround ourselves with people with whom we can collaborate for mutual success, we are creating a village. These may be people who live close to us physically, or they may be people with whom we associate at church or work or in social circles, or both. Either way, if they are committed to helping us and our loved ones to thrive, and we are likewise committed to them, then the village is essentially a reality. But like any village, this kind requires some effort to define and maintain.

There's a need to spend time together, and to share common values, and to communicate effectively, and to plan and organize structured learning opportunities and rites of passage for children. There is an obligation to share resources and information and to keep track of noteworthy events in the larger communities of which the new villages are a part. There's a requirement to network with other villages for strength, support and safety. There is much to do. It is not easy to create and maintain a village in a world that largely considers them an anachronism; but doing so is essential to all we hope to gain.

Needless to say, raising children has to be a priority for every village. A uniquely defined success for all of our children is the foundation for our tomorrows as well as a critical element in the fabric of our todays. How well we are able to bring them to maturity is critical to the survival of the world we live in and an absolute prerequisite for any thriving we hope to do while on this earth. We must set our children firmly on the road to becoming fully developed human beings or our mediocrity as a species is ensured. That takes a serious, long-term commitment.

Yet, when we define what a child is, perhaps we should include all of us. None of us ever get to the end of the road that takes us toward being fully developed humans. As the saying goes, "life is a journey—not a destination." We have to work together constantly to move each and every one of us further and further along the road to self-actualization and cooperative planetary citizenship. We are never fully raised, and without a sense of the village we may not even get <u>close</u> to the maturity of which we are capable.

Unfortunately, we have apparently come to believe some pretty strange things about human procreation. One of these strange beliefs is that good parenting occurs as an automatic outgrowth of success in biologically producing a child. It seems many of us think we are supposed to just instinctively know what it takes to raise children successfully.

A second, and equally disturbing belief, is our certainty that we have a mandate to go it alone, to achieve parental stardom without a smidgen of help from someone else. That's sad, but fortunately, it's not a terminal attitude.

The good news is that we collectively know a lot about parenting and community building and communication and a host of other things that make it possible for us to thrive. The bad news is that until and unless we recreate villages to help raise children for success, we will continue to flounder in a huge, unmanageable world that scoffs at the meager efforts toward thriving that we are able to muster on our own.

It takes a village to raise us all. It always has; and it always will. Such is the nature of society. If we're smart we'll learn to redefine and recreate villages for the coming centuries.

PRIVILEGE AND RESPONSIBILITY

In a lovely parable called The Laws of Spirit, author Dan Millman writes, "…you can learn the Law of Compassion from the Earth on whose skin we tread, whose trees we cut and burn, whose living wealth we exploit, going about our business without ever thinking of asking permission or giving thanks." I hope he's right about what we can learn because he is definitely right about the attitude we often take toward the blessings of our lives.

Once a year, we celebrate a holiday we call Thanksgiving. On that occasion, at least, we may pause to reflect on the enormity of our privilege. We feast; and honor our families; and take a break from work; and celebrate with parades, sports events, and television specials; and engage in a variety of activities that are steeped in custom and tradition. For a variety of reasons, there are exceptions to this rule; but they only serve to prove the rule. And yet, this wonderful, nationwide festival can ring hollow.

One of the greatest errors we make is to confuse the term "privilege" with what is meant by the word "right." I think they are very different. The world owes us certain rights, but it only allows us our prerogatives.

I am reminded of the rhetoric of our country's Declaration of Independence, which declares that "all men are created equal" and "endowed by their Creator with certain unalienable rights" among which are "life, liberty and the *pursuit* of happiness." We have the right to live, and be free and to make our best effort to be happy, but if we achieve any degree of happiness, that is a favor we are allowed—not a right.

In America and many other countries, we each probably destroy, misuse, overuse or waste more resources in a single day than some individuals even have access to within a single week. Famine, drought, poverty, hunger and malnutrition are very real challenges for millions of people in the world. There are places where there is little or no food, or water, or shelter or money to purchase these bare essentials of life when they are existent.

Then again, there are places where resources may be readily available, but some power-hungry government refuses to allow people access. There are places where lack of knowledge is the true deficit and access to the right information or skills could make the difference between life and death for many people. Happiness hardly enters the picture.

Then there are folks like you and me. Consider, for a moment just how favored we are. Even some of the poorest in America often have more resources at their disposal than the wealthiest in some other societies. And when we consider average Americans, it's probably a good choice of words to say, "at our disposal." Altogether, we will likely throw away the annual gross national product of some underdeveloped countries between sunrise and sunset today. Our rate of consumption is appalling enough; but our rate of waste is (in a word) disgusting.

When we bask in the afterglow of our feasting from time to time, let's remember those who experience famine. As we enjoy the right to pursue our happiness in a free country, let's not forget world citizens who are yet in some form of bondage. As we relish a nation where the only bombs that explode are those set off by terrorists, criminals, movie-makers and soldiers in training, let's keep in mind those for whom war is a constant threat or a very real terror. As we celebrate with our beloved friends and relatives, let's try to recall those who have had loved ones snatched away by violence and other misfortunes. As we experience the joys and comforts of our homes, let's be certain to keep in mind that there are so many who have no homes.

Most of all, please don't lose sight of the fact that our thoughts, and words and prayers are nothing if they are not matched with deeds. We must use the platform of our privilege to launch campaigns of responsibility toward those less fortunate. At the very least, we should do everything within our power to extend the promise of democracy to everyone: the rights of life, liberty and the pursuit of happiness. Only then can we begin to insure for everyone a providence that can emerge from those rights.

FROM PENNIES TO MILLIONS
(PEOPLE HELPING PEOPLE)

Imagine this: If we randomly selected some person who lives in this country without a penny to call his own, and we all gave him one, he would be a millionaire more than twice over.

Now think about this: If we contributed in this way to the Millionaireship of a <u>million people</u> it would cost us less than many of us pay for a late model used car: $10,000.

Now consider this: If all of us helped each other in times of need in a little bit more focused and caring way, would any of us have to want for anything that we really needed? Somehow, I think there is something terribly wrong with the picture of some Americans living in luxurious opulence while others live in penurious pestilence.

Please understand, though, that I'm not troubled by people gaining wealth. I sincerely hope and plan to gain more of my own. I'm just troubled by the same thing that bothered Karl Marx; the rich keep getting richer, while the poor get poorer. But don't think I'm going to start espousing communism or socialism over capitalism. I believe I'm a capitalist through and through. I just believe in <u>altruistic</u> capitalism.

Do you understand that the reason United Way works is because united is the way it works? When people give just a little of themselves and their substance towards a common goal, the goal is more easily and painlessly reached. When people selfishly hoard their wares, those who are less fortunate suffer needlessly.

Do you gather that multi-level marketing works because the marketers gather level-headed, multifaceted individuals who are all willing to give a little bit of their time, energy and substance so everyone participating can eventually have an abundance of these things?

Do you see that one seed out of hundreds that may be produced by a plant can lead to hundreds more plants just like the one that produced the single seed?

In each of these cases, choosing to sacrifice a little bit for a big purpose leads to a harvest of plenty. Give pleasantly with purpose and you cannot help but receive gratefully with pleasance. Ancient (and universal) wisdom has long told us that we "reap what we sow;" "that it is more blessed to give than receive;" that what you give out comes back to you.

Give out your kindness. Give out your generosity. Give out your assistance. Give out your energy. Give out your resources. Give out your time. Give out your love. It will all come back…(sooner or later; one way or another) just like it went out…but better. And if you do it with purpose, you will be fulfilling one of yours.

WELFARE OR "WELL FAIR?"
(HANDOUTS VS. HANDS UP)

The term "well" might be defined as "a device used to tap an underground supply." The word "fair," in one context, means "just and honest;" in another, it means "favorable or helpful;" in still another, it is an "exhibition" or "exposition." When we combine the two terms to create a new term spelled w-e-l-l-f-a-i-r, perhaps we get to a definition of what "w-e-l-f-a-r-e" ought to be.

Our new "wellfair" (with the new spelling) would be "a just, honest and favorable system to help tap the underground supply of talents and abilities that all people can expose or exhibit to help others as they help themselves." Now there's something that makes sense! I think anybody would want to trade this for what welfare is and has been for a long time.

First of all, there has been a lot of injustice and dishonesty in the current system...on the part of some of the administrators as well as some of the recipients. And "favorable" is not a word that can be favorably applied to most aspects of this self-perpetuating dependency. There is a negative stigma attached to people who receive benefits, to people who must approve or disapprove them, and to the system itself—even among those who apparently profit.

Secondly, there is little in the current system that is designed to "tap the underground supply of talents and abilities that all people can expose or exhibit." Many people targeted by the current welfare system could work and would work diligently if they had opportunity and proper guidance to discover and develop skills that are significantly marketable. Like everyone else, they want to be able to provide for themselves and their families in a dignified and respectful manner and make meaningful contributions to society. From the moment they are born, however, (and for whatever reasons) the liquid assets of their inner lives have been draining out at a rate that dwarfs the influx of self-actualization from both inside and outside sources.

As for providing opportunities for welfare clients to help others while they help themselves, the current system does almost none of the first and (arguably) very little of the second. The current benefit structure does not provide the time, energy, or resources for recipients to do much more than simply survive from day to day. And mere survival is certainly not the "end-all and be-all" of what human being is about. Welfare families are "helped" to a degree; but they cannot truly help others or themselves.

Perhaps we'll fare well with "well-fair" if we welcome it into our awareness, but we need to welcome something like it into our society as well. It would be fair to say that more of our underprivileged citizens could exhibit a greater degree of wellness if we set about claiming (or reclaiming) the lost potential of people in the same way we would for any other lost wealth.

Like diamonds in the rough, talented people must be discovered, shaped and polished so that their many facets of capability can shine through. Understandably, this takes a willingness to focus the time, energy, effort, cooperation and resources necessary for thousands of human habilitation and reclamation projects. We cannot depend on government to do this. We can and should do it ourselves.

In the words of a well-known song, "each one can reach one." And if we all did, maybe no one would have to suffer the indignity of the paradoxical trap of not being able to help themselves because they can't (or don't know how to) help themselves to help themselves. We must stop giving people handouts and give them hands up instead.

AN APB FOR RITES OF PASSAGE
(OH, WHERE... OH, WHERE HAVE OUR CEREMONIES GONE?)

I'd like to borrow a strategy from law enforcement officials and declare an APB—an "all-points bulletin. I'm not looking for an escaped convict, however. I'm also not looking for a burglar, a bank robber, a bond jumper or a runaway. What I'd like to find (with help from all of you) is a universal rite of passage for our children.

The Jewish community perpetuates one of the world's most brilliant examples of rites of passage for young people with a continuing commitment to Bar- and Bat-Mitzvahs. These ceremonies publicly recognize young people who are emerging into adulthood; but not only are they recognized, they are trained and otherwise prepared to be contributing members of the total Jewish community and to maintain the strengths and traditions of their forefathers.

There are other scattered pockets of American society where rites of passage are ceremoniously observed and diligently preserved for posterity. Some Mexican-Americans, for example, still observe "Sweet Sixteen" parties for their young women and in some African-American communities, a program called "Rites of Passage" has been instituted. But this does not eliminate the total problem. They are, after all, still scattered practices. Where is the preparation for and recognition of imminent adulthood for the average American adolescent? Frankly, the answer is NOWHERE.

It is no wonder, then, that teenagers in the U.S. (and elsewhere) must struggle to find their own ways to be recognized as adults; and their efforts often have disastrous results. The statistics for teenage pregnancy and parenthood, alcoholism and drug abuse, drinking and driving, rape and robbery, and assault and murder are staggering. Whether with assorted crimes and punishments, or with various other misguided choices and their terrible consequences young people are stumbling (or crashing) into an adulthood that they are not prepared for and which is not prepared for them. And often when troubled teens are pressed to explain their troubling choices, they talk about "getting respect;" or they say that "no one cares;" or they make declarations like "I just wanted someone to love me;" or they say that "no one understands what we're going through."

What we need are some observers, some dreamers, some lovers and some workers—but not necessarily in that order, and not necessarily packaged in different bodies. But we do need one or more persons who can clearly see the need for legitimate and viable rites of passage for American youth. Then they need to be able to dream of a way for every child to access a "coming of age" process and ceremony that is appropriate for them and for the community of which they will become an integral part. Next, they need to care enough about kids in general (and some kids in particular) that they are compelled to make a difference. Finally, they need to be able to devote enough time and energy to work toward establishing a momentum that will carry rites of passage firmly into our collective future.

On the other hand, maybe we just need folks to roll up their sleeves and start meeting more of the needs that young people have. From that kind of beginning, perhaps appropriate rites of passage will emerge. What are the chances that you are one of the people we are all looking for?

YOUTH EMPLOYMENT
(A MEANINGFUL OPPORTUNITY KIDS AND FAMILIES NEED)

When American society was largely agrarian and about 90% of its citizens lived on farms and only the remainder in metropolitan areas, large families were also more of the norm. Children, then, were more of an asset than a liability. The extra hands were needed to perform the extensive list of tasks that were necessary for the family to sustain itself and perhaps even to generate extra income.

Even as the Industrial Revolution began its inexorable rise to prominence in society and the economy, family survival was often dependent on the combined efforts of every able-bodied person in the family. Children sometimes worked as long and hard as their parents did to contribute wages to the family's economic gain.

Thankfully, laws were passed (in America if not elsewhere) to prevent the exploitation of the innocent by the unscrupulous. Otherwise, (among other things) greedy and calloused business and factory owners would have thoughtlessly (and sometimes brutally) destroyed the lives of children in blind pursuit of the almighty dollar—just as some still do in "sweatshops" worldwide. Unfortunately, however, the pendulum of youth employment in developed countries like ours may have swung too far in the other direction.

In today's society, children are often more of a liability than an asset. The family enterprise or farm is mostly a thing of the past. The extra helping hands that were once indispensable in families are often idle now; but the extra mouths to feed, bodies to clothe, minds to educate, and well nesses to maintain are still there. And many times, there are far more of these extras than there should be thanks to a lack of family planning.

Perhaps human nature—in the case of procreation—should be set on a different course than what it normally takes. Obviously, having large families in today's society puts a lot more pressure on the family breadwinners. And in more and more families, there is only one of those. Often it is a mother whose earning power is (unfortunately) still far less than it might be if she were the father instead.

This whole dynamic is a far more complicated situation than we can adequately explore here and now; but one of the remedies that can begin to make a positive difference is for our communities to find a way to appropriately and gainfully employ our youth. We never want to return to the days when some would exploit children for monetary gain; but we have no choice in these days but to employ youth for societal gain.

Finding ways to put able-bodied, energetic, idle-minded, and basically altruistic children to work (even if the work is unpaid) keeps many of them off the streets, out of trouble, and engaged in learning about the many dynamics of rewards received for energies expended. Where wealth is earned, however, common sense dictates that it should also be shared with those who help produce it. It's too bad that this kind of common sense is so uncommon.

Finding employment for kids helps the children, it helps their families, and it ultimately helps society. It is to our great advantage to find more and more ways to do it. Please consider how you can contribute to that.

DO WHAT YOU CAN,
FOR WHOM YOU CAN, WHILE YOU CAN

Because of the personal and vocational circles I'm in, I often encounter people in helping professions. Sometimes I find them quite stressed by their challenges. When this is the case, whether or not they are educators, counselors, social workers, therapists, law enforcement officials, attorneys, healers, ministers or whatever doesn't seem to matter nearly as much as how deeply they are committed to genuinely helping people.

Fortunately, most of the helpers I know or meet really are committed. In fact, some of them are so devoted, there are times when I think they should be committed—if you catch my drift.

The danger of incredible levels of devotion to helping others is that those who have it are often overwhelmed by the enormity of the collective needs of the populations they want to serve. There is so much need and only limited amounts of the helper's time, energy, and resources that can be applied to meeting the need.

For folks who are in this dilemma, I have developed an aphorism that I hope encourages them while helping to keep them healthy and sane. I say to them, "Do WHAT you can, for WHOM you can, WHILE you can, and know when you CANNOT!" As time permits, I try to explain what that means to me and what I hope it will mean to them. For the times when you are one of those helpers, I'd like to do the same for you.

To do what you can means just that…and no more. The problem for lots of us helpers is that we want to do more than we can. I try to remind folks that if they are doing their best, no one—including themselves—can expect more from them than that. If they are giving less than their best, it usually has very little to do with their desire to do well but a lot to do with their current ability. But that's another issue and we'll come to that in a moment.

Doing what you can means doing what you have the power to do. Each of us has unique combinations of talents, and abilities, and skills, and unique opportunities to apply them in our experience. As we use them, we sharpen the capabilities and, as a result, become more capable. That's good news; so go ahead and use what you have and do what you can. That's the ticket! No more. No less.

Doing for <u>whom</u> you can is also governed by opportunities and limits and challenges. There will always be those that we cannot help. There are some poor souls with whom we will not come in contact. Others will not have our help, perhaps, because we will not choose to support those workers who <u>do</u> come in contact with them. Still others will miss having our assistance because they will arrive at a time when we are completely tapped out, in the process of helping others (or ourselves), or when we are preparing to do so.

Sometimes we just have to say, "I'm really sorry; but I just can't help you right now," and refer them to another helper (or another time.)

To do for whom you can also means to take advantage of the legitimate opportunities you have to render aid and to realize that those you help necessarily displace many others who may need you as much. It's important to understand that.

We must also remember to tell people when we <u>cannot</u> help (even if it's because we don't want to for some reason) and to be really careful about how we prioritize responding to needs. We must allow people the dignity of feeling that we value them and the importance of what they require. We must be wise enough to know when we can relegate them to less than a top priority—and when we cannot.

To help others <u>while</u> you can means a lot. It's about opportunity, energy, resources, priorities, self-care, preparation, abilities, and more.

We mustn't kick ourselves for the opportunities we don't get to help others. We are sometimes just not in the right place at the right time. We may run out of energy or resources and simply be depleted when the need arises. We may be the wrong helper for the right need (or the right helper for the wrong need—or the wrong time). We may not be prepared, not have the right skills, or not be available because we are taking care of ourselves or other priorities. Sometimes there are things we cannot do.

For the things we can do, however, we must remember to remind ourselves: "Do what you can, for whom you can, while you can, and know when you cannot."

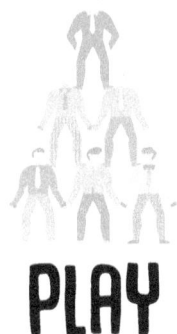

PLAY

(KEEPING THE INNER CHILD ALIVE AND HAPPY)

D o you remember when you used to play? If you're smart, you never stopped; but most of us do, you know—at least to some extent. If work is not play for us, a lot of us hardly play at all.

When we were growing up, we engaged in play for the sake of play. There were no ulterior motives, no dark purposes, no Freudian intentions—just pure unadulterated fun and a whole lot of incidental learning. And all it required was a prop or two, one or more other kids (if they were handy), and maybe a few rules. With these very modest requirements fulfilled, it took about three seconds to start a game of jump-rope, hopscotch, "Mother, May I," Hide and Go Seek, jacks, marbles, Cops and Robbers, Cowboys and Indians, or mud pies. Do you remember those things?

Do you remember Kick The Can, stick-ball, Barbies, playing house, back-yard baseball, checkers, dominoes, Old Maid…Spin The Bottle? I'll bet that you do. But do you have any idea where the little person went that used to do all those things?

Whatever happened to the little kid you used to be? As you got older, more sophisticated (and if you're really lucky—wiser and more mature), what happened to the child you were? Is that kid still alive? If it's alive, is it happy?

Whoever said that you had to give up all your "kid stuff" in order to be a "grown-up"? Who decided that to be an adult, one has to lock away or murder the child in himself or herself that a person has come to know and love? Why do we have to so completely trade one world for the other?

In the Bible's book Ecclesiastes, there is a passage that says, "To everything, there is a season and a time to every purpose under the heavens." When it comes to matters of maturation, most of us would interpret that to mean that there is a time for being a kid and a time for being a "big people" and never the twain shall meet. Who says?

That Biblical passage doesn't tell us when the times and seasons should be? Why not make a little time every day or week or month to open up the doors of your heart, mind and soul and invite your little kid to come out and play? Contrary to popular belief, the little rascal is not dead—even if you've tried to kill it.

And since we have already touched on a Biblical theme, we might as well comment on another passage you might find familiar. In the thirteenth chapter of 1st Corinthians, Paul writes "When I was a child, I spake as a child, I understood as a child, I thought as a child; but when I became a man, I put away childish things." Now you may disagree with me, but I think the word play is conspicuous by its absence in this verse. Speaking, understanding and thinking are far different from playing.

By the way, you can ask any little kid in the world (and a bunch of teenagers) what it takes to have fun, and they won't mention alcohol, tobacco or other drugs; they won't mention sexual activity; they will seldom if ever speak of money; and they won't normally tell you that it requires expensive manufactured toys or other playthings. When do we forget what the young ones so clearly understand?

And what about things like hugs, and tears, and laughter and the exhaustion that comes from play at a maddening pace? And what about wonder, and surprise, and questions, and amazements, and creativity, and daydreaming? Where do those things go for so many of us? And what about biking, and dancing, and making up songs, and just being silly without worrying about what others think? What about just being yourself?

Perhaps one more Biblical reference is a good place to end our meditation on play. In the nineteenth chapter of Matthew (and elsewhere), Jesus is quoted as saying. "Suffer little children, and forbid them not, to come unto me; for of such is the kingdom of heaven."

If we do no more than interpret the word "heaven" in this excerpt as a synonym for joy, we would do well to remember that the defining activity for children is play. They don't define themselves by work, and careers, and roles, and rules, and relationships. They anchor their identity and shape their world-view through play. And even when they play at being "grown-up", they allow themselves to be a lot more creative than the adults after which they model.

Give yourself a break. Even if it lasts a hundred years, life is too short (or maybe too long) to spend it being so deathly serious for most of it. PLAY!

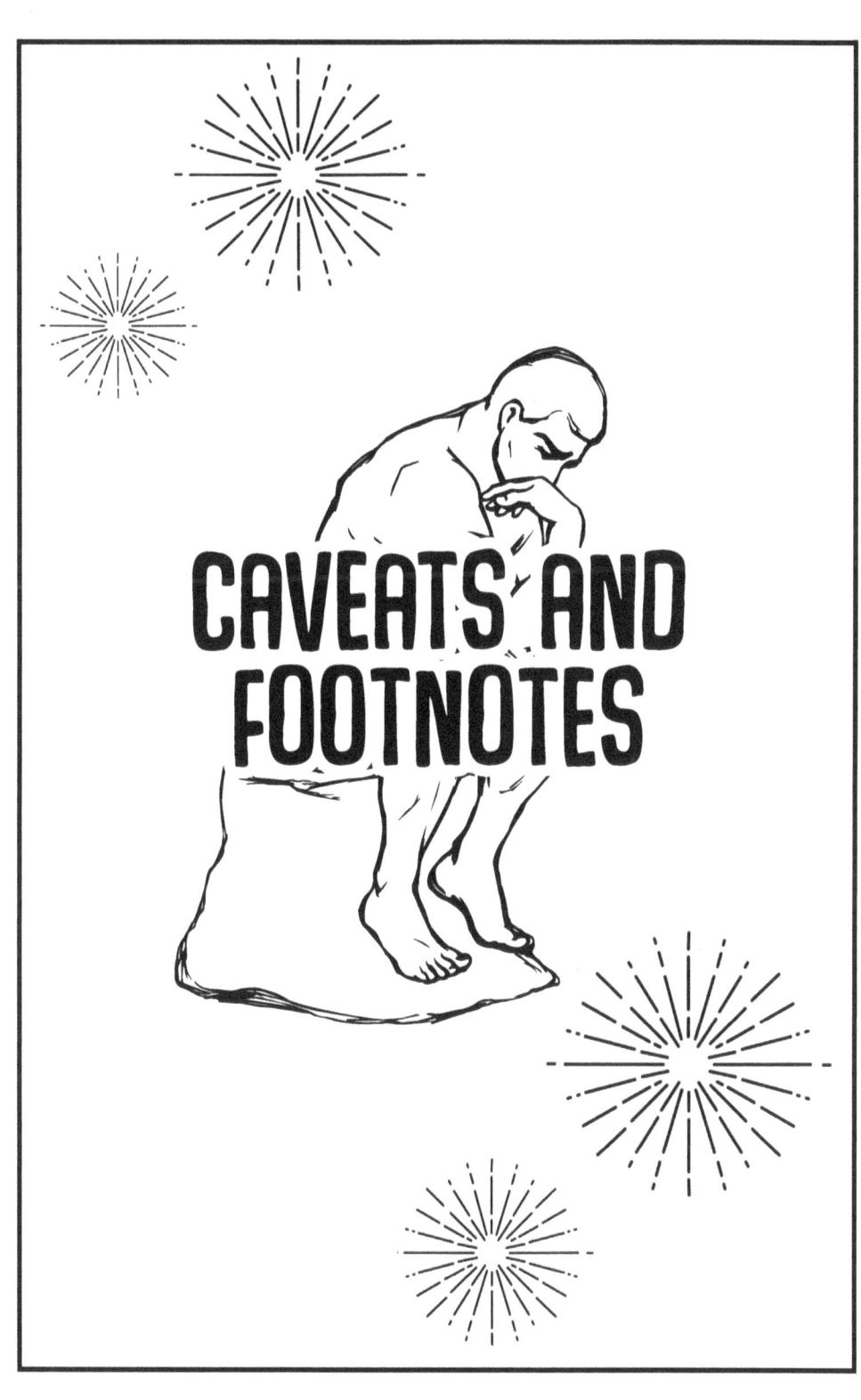

BOOMERANG

Throw a boomerang,
And it flies back at you.
It might even bang
Your head-bone black and blue!

Almost anything
You "throw" like that in life,
Could some comfort bring
(Or cut you like a knife!)

One can't know for sure
What rebounds will take place—
Whether deeds are pure
Or fallen far from grace.

Even ricochets
Of actions that you do
Could bounce other ways
And still come back to you.

Physics law tidbits
Remind us that for acts,
Equal opposites
Occur. (Those are the facts.)

Karma, too, asserts
(By laws that govern it)
That good deeds and hurts
We do create a pit.

Sure to fall inside,
We're smart to have it lined—
Not with spikes pit-wide—
But with soft down...in-kind.

Hey..."What goes around...
It comes around," we hear.
Wise men often found
The truth of that was clear.

My analysis:
(For those who give a hang)
Take care what you send,
For it's a boomerang.

EITHER/OR; OR AND/AND?
(AVOIDING THE DICHOTOMOUS TRAP)

"Either/or" thinking is often a dangerous trap. If something is either black or white, it denies the existence of gray. If something is either right or wrong, it begs the question of, "By whose standards?" If something is either "up" or "down," we must ask from what perspective that judgment is made. Consider locations in the void of space where such directions are meaningless!

Perspective and perception are always deciding factors in judgments about phenomena of all kinds. Yet, we must remember that as similar as these two words sound, they are very different.

Perspective is about <u>point</u> of view. Figuratively speaking, it is the place you stand when you look at the world around you. Perception, on the other hand, is about <u>quality</u> of view. It is about clarity of vision. It is about getting an understanding that is hopefully unsullied by prejudicial thoughts and feelings. But the two of them, together, are the parents of nearly all observations of events, appearances, and circumstances. That's why when we decide that something—anything—is either this or that, we can easily fall into a trap from which it is nearly impossible to successfully extricate ourselves.

I prefer what I like to call the "and/and" solution. It is possible, for instance, for something to be black and white—even if it's not a Jersey cow, a zebra, a newspaper, or medium gray in color. A fair example of that is a photographic negative of a black and white snapshot taken with a camera. It all depends on your perspective.

A better example would be the viewpoint of people who are totally blind or in total darkness. Is it not true that without the benefit of light or the gift of physical vision, everything may appear black to these folks? It's a matter of perception.

I'm also reminded of a story (or perhaps it is a parable) about an alleged question on an intelligence test where the query was, "What color is a banana?" The correct answer was presumed to be "yellow," when, in fact, the legitimate answer could be "green" if it's not yet ripe, "brown," if it is overly ripe, and "black," if it has become compost.

Every dichotomy—up/down, right/wrong, in/out, good/bad, Liberal/Conservative, saint/sinner, intelligent/ignorant, and many more—is an absolute offspring of perspective and perception. Unless we learn that perspective and perception colors every opinion about "the way things are," we will forever be victims of our tendency toward "either/or" thinking. Our only hope is to legitimize "and/and" reasoning.

A point on a map may be up if you are looking at it from a place to the South of it; but it could always be down for anyone who lives at a higher elevation. It's "up" and "down." Killing another human being is considered wrong if it's cold-blooded murder; but the same judges might consider it right if it's in a war. Killing, then, is possibly both "right" and "wrong."

I think you get the picture. But that really depends on your current perspective and perception of these words. This either makes sense, or it doesn't. Or perhaps we should say it makes sense and it doesn't. Take your pick. But make sure you pick the "right" one, okay?

Oops...

FIGHT, FLIGHT OR FLOW
(ANOTHER OPTION IN OUR REFLEXIVE CHOICES)

When the seed of an idea comes into my awareness, I'm always grateful. When it's a seed that blossoms into great fruit, I'm even more thankful. And in the latter case, I'm also inclined to remember who planted the seed.

My friend, Galen Davis, was responsible for one of these prolific seeds. One day in conversation, he casually dropped in a perspective about dealing with stress that stood out for me then and has stuck with me since.

Galen said that it made sense to him that we consider adding a third option to the choices available in what we know as the "Fight or Flight Syndrome." He advocated that we think in terms of "Fight, Flight or Flow, as in "go with the flow." In my opinion he is absolutely right in this perception; and I don't know that it can be any more succinctly stated.

Most of us are no doubt familiar with the "fight or flight" jargon. The purveyors of insights into the psyche have long used this terminology to help us understand the causes of stress. Theoretically, the basic human creature that's within each of us is still programmed to respond to perceived danger by either fighting or taking flight to protect itself.

When there is a legitimate danger to us in the physical realm, these options still make sense. If an aggressive animal attacks us, we may fight it off with a club or stick. If a runaway vehicle is suddenly bearing down on us as we walk down the street, we will no doubt try to jump or run out of the way.

But what happens when the dangers are less tangible? What if there is no apparent enemy to fight? What if the peril exists only in our minds?

What if we are threatened by our own thoughts and feelings? What if we have nothing to fear but fear itself? When any of these things are true, the option of "flow" makes sense in a way that the other options cannot.

One thing about being a human that's challenging is that part of us is animal and responds instinctively in the way an animal would. The problem with that is that when we don't have outlets for the energy that rises up to motivate our battles or our avoidance behaviors, the pent-up energy starts to do measurable damage to our minds and bodies. The release of that energy, when it mounts up, is imperative.

Exercise, relaxation, diversion and other strategies are good for shutting off that would-be protective energy when it builds; but perhaps an even better strategy, at times, is to open ourselves to channeling or deflecting it harmlessly away. Such is the nature of flow. Rather than bracing against the onslaught of negative energies, we can find ways to let them flow through us the same way the powerful energy of electricity can be allowed to flow through a conduit.

Safe and effective methods for going with the flow are many and varied. We won't take time to examine very many of them here and now. Perhaps what's more important in these moments is to fully recognize that there is another very viable option. When troubles come our way, not only can we fight or take flight, but we can also (and perhaps more effectively) go with the flow.

Go with the flow....
Go with the flow....
Go with the flow....
Go with the flow....

CONDITIONAL EXPECTATIONS
(OUR RELUCTANCE TO SUSPEND JUDGMENT AND SELFISHNESS)

An affirmation from Karen Wylie suggests that we love unconditionally and not try to control or manipulate in order to make the world meet our expectations. And, of course, you know we have expectations!

We have expectations about safety, about propriety, about morality, about self-control. We have expectations about leadership, and decision-making, and the status quo. We have expectations about the economy, world trade, immigration, work, retirement, family, and neighbors. In short, we have expectations about everything; and along with our expectations come conditions.

We expect a world full of largely uncontrollable variables to be completely safe, and when we find that it's not we retreat into paranoia, overreaction, and sometimes what psychologists call anal behavior. We expect our leaders to be infallible, and when we discover they are not we publicly vilify them. Never mind that we wouldn't want the same thing to happen to us.

When we make mistakes, it's not our fault. When others make mistakes, it's entirely their fault. When we experience unpleasant consequences as a result of our actions, it's because of circumstances beyond our control. When others experience unpleasant consequences for their actions, they had it coming because they have no self-control. How comfortable we are with our double standards!

We want things to change at the same time that we want things to stay the same. We avoid making important decisions like the plague and then get upset when others make decisions in our stead that we don't like. We want prosperity for all, but we seem to have no idea that universal prosperity cannot co-exist with selfish hoarding and unbridled consumption. We want to freely buy and sell abroad, and to have the opportunity to live wherever we want, but we don't want to afford the same privilege to others. Many of us have no fluency in a second language, but we insist that those whose native tongue is different than ours learn the language that <u>we</u> speak. We want to enjoy a comfortable retirement, but we won't discipline ourselves to save for it. We have conditions for our expectations, and many are at least unspoken if not completely unrealized.

What we probably should learn and remember is to severely limit or (better yet) <u>eliminate</u> our expectations, suspend our judgments, and realize we cannot impose our conditions on a world that will not be tamed. On the other hand, as we have explored before, we can certainly have desires and goals and affirmations, but we must allow for the powers that be in the universe to manifest our destinies in ways that we usually have little developed capacity to imagine.

Meanwhile if we can just learn to abandon our need to manipulate outcomes, so many of the circumstances we seek to control might not be nearly as detrimental as we might at first believe. It's like the parable that teaches us to consider that a destination down a rushing river might be more quickly and easily reached if we dive into the water than if we trudge the path along the river's banks. There are certainly issues of safety in such a choice, but what if you <u>have</u> no choice? What if you <u>fall</u> in? What if you were <u>born</u> into the flow of the river?

There is a flow to life that makes sense in ways we cannot yet fully fathom; but the effort we expend trying to <u>control</u> that flow could perhaps be much better spent trying to <u>understand</u> it and to determine where it goes. Increasingly it seems to be going along a path that is practically indistinguishable from a love without condition for all people, for who we really <u>are,</u> <u>where</u> we are, and what happens as we experience life together. It's that flow thing again. Maybe the way the Universe is unfolding is as it should be after all and needs no interference from us (and our sensibilities about how things <u>should</u> be). To allow that to be as it may is daring, of course, but it is also a risk when we do not. And when we look at where our conditional expectations about the world have taken us, can we be sure that it is not better to avoid constant control and manipulation of circumstances?

HIDDEN AGENDAS
(OR "HOW SNEAKY CAN FOLKS GET?")

There are a lot of things going on in our world. Some result from the inexorable process of evolution—of life, of thought and of the Universe, itself. Inevitably, there is change for change's sake. But some of what is happening is the direct result of people making conscious (and sometimes unconscious) choices.

From various political and ideological corners, along the way, we have witnessed the emergence of Newt Gingrich and The New Republicans; the phenomenon of Louis Farrakhan and The "Million Man March;" a U. N. visit by the much reviled yet seemingly untouchable Fidel Castro; the continuing saber-rattling of Iraq's Saddam Hussein, and unprecedented terrorist attacks on American soil. It seems like everyone has something to say and something they want to do.

From uniquely American places on the "Map of Many Viewpoints" come folks like Phyllis Schlafly; Mark Fuhrman; Anita Hill; Jerry Jones; Jesse Jackson; Maya Angelou; Rush Limbaugh; Spike Lee; Janet Reno; Colin Powell; Sarah Brady; and rapper, Snoop Doggy Dog. It appears that everyone has something to say and something they want to do.

On the landscape of ideology, you find Fundamentalists, Leftists, Rightists, Centrists, radicals, wafflers, Constitutionalists, civil libertarians, literalists, fence-sitters, Conservatives, Liberals, Moderates, degenerates, lunatics and "none of the above." Some fall into these camps by their own admission, some by being christened that way by those who are not. Either way, the labels don't tell us much at all about the people behind them or what they really want. Apparently, everyone has something they want to say and do. The problem is that the two are often not in perfect harmony.

For this very reason, the word rhetoric has a negative connotation with many people. For as long as people have actively sought to persuade others through the use of language (which is what rhetoric really is) there have been people who would <u>say one</u> thing and <u>do</u> another. When the "walk" doesn't match the "talk," we understandably have a real problem with the talk. What's worse is that by the time we discover the incongruity, someone has figuratively (and perhaps literally) walked all over us, or someone else.

It is sad, but true, that many of us have learned to take every message that comes our way with a whole <u>teaspoon</u> of salt. A grain of salt doesn't get it anymore. We've been duped too many times by the hidden agenda. We've been suckered too many times by those who speak with "forked tongue." We've been disappointed far too often by those who <u>say one</u> thing and <u>do</u> another; who <u>claim</u> one thing but <u>want</u> another; who <u>ask</u> us for one thing while they secretly <u>take</u> something else; who want us to believe <u>one</u> thing about them when (if the truth be told) they are very <u>different</u> than what they profess—or even what they believe.

Now, you may be thinking this has nothing to do with you and choices you make. If so, you might want to think again. The chances are really good that we are all guilty of this sin from time to time and to one degree or another. But the <u>degrees</u> really matter.

It's one thing to lie profusely to preserve the "surprise" in a surprise birthday party; that is forgivable. It's quite another to lie profusely to preserve a semblance of humanity in one who epitomizes "man's inhumanity to man." If most of us fall somewhere on a continuum from one of these extremes to the other, hopefully, most of us are a lot closer to the surprise party end. Meanwhile, I suspect those dangerously close to the other end are the ones who will victimize the rest of us.

I wish I had an answer for us; but I don't. Part of me wants to trust everyone and believe that they are ultimately motivated by the best of virtues; but I am not so naive. Another part of me wants to <u>mis</u>trust everyone and count on the fact that they are selfish, greedy and callous. I'm not that naive either.

Somewhere in the middle, I try to be observant, intuitive, proactive, diplomatic, communicative, congruent, and unconditionally loving. And that's the <u>best</u> advice I can give <u>you.</u>

THE TRAP OF ROUTINES
(OR "HOW TO AVOID A FALSE SENSE OF SECURITY)

There's something to be said for having a routine. Routines are comfortable. Routines are predictable. Routines are dependable. But routines are NOT infallible. They are fine until some contingency comes along, catches you napping, and puts the proverbial monkey wrench in your routine plans. At that point you realize that nothing is ever really routine—at least not in the way we'd like to think.

Even for someone who experiences every day as <u>different</u>, it is possible to be lulled into a false sense of security by the sameness of <u>expected</u> surprises. You may even start to think that no surprise can shock you until you <u>are</u> shocked by the surprise you could never have anticipated, or the inattention you could never have imagined.

Have you ever seen a batter in a baseball game strike out and then look at his bat as if he expects to find a six-inch hole in it? Or how about the basketball player who flubs a cross-court pass from a teammate, watches it sail out of bounds as if it had a mind of its own, and then shakes her head as if the event was about as inexplicable as the entire arena suddenly disappearing before her eyes.

It's the kind of incredulity that can only exist when you've done a thing a thousand times. It can only happen when some function is second nature to you. It can only occur when you have repeated an operation so often that you could almost do it in your sleep. You can only be that surprised when you have been victimized by your own routine.

Many of us who lead busy, productive lives are like jugglers who can keep more than a handful of things in a delicate balance of motion all at once. We juggle schedules and responsibilities and contingencies and crises and occasionally may even dispassionately marvel at our ability to do so. Then once in a while we drop something—maybe something really important—and we are suddenly confused, and incredulous, and self-deprecating, and apologetic, and maybe terribly sad, or angry with ourselves, or the circumstances, or both.

Normally, we can handle all of this just fine, we say. Usually, things are kept under control. We almost always manage quite well, we surmise. "How could this happen?" we ask. Though we may well understand the foibles of being human, a part of us still longs for the perfection that will prevent our mistakes, eliminate our disappointments, destroy our shortcomings, and shield our vulnerability. We keep trying to perfect our routines in an effort to perfect our achievements. We fail because we're human—and less than perfect—no matter how unfailing we think we may be in certain areas.

I think the point in all of this (once again) is for us to remind ourselves that we cannot do better than our best and that sometimes our best efforts won't be good enough for what we intend to accomplish. We have to forgive ourselves for the human frailty that sometimes allows or compels us to drop the ball, or miss the pitch, or get hit by bullets we usually dodge.

Most of all, when we encounter those who may somehow be victims of their own routines, may we all be strong enough (at least sometimes) to grace them with forgiveness if they have trouble forgiving themselves for their faux pas. If we can, maybe the balance of nature will bring or return that favor to us when we need it most. I sure hope so. Otherwise, when I disappoint those who are counting on me when I have dropped the ball; unless they are magnanimous, it may be a long time before I can experience forgiveness. Those I disappoint can usually forgive me long before I can forgive myself.

I'm sure that I, too, must learn that sometimes I will be responsible for my own snafus for which I will need to be responsible for my own forgiveness. In military parlance, "snafu" is a slang term that (euphemistically speaking) is an abbreviation for "situation normal, all fouled up." What a perfect description for a routine that fails us!

THE OBSESSION WITH CONVENIENCE

(A CASE FOR MAKING A LITTLE EFFORT NOW AND THEN)

must admit that I enjoy certain conveniences as much as anyone; but I am not obsessed with them, and I seldom choose a convenience simply because I'm too lazy to make a little effort. In fact, because I am highly motivated to get things done that are important to me, I most often try to surround myself with conveniences that make my work easier, which save me time for accomplishing appointed tasks, or which are practical in some way.

For an example, around my house, I'm known as "Gadget Man" by my wife and son because I love finding functional and convenient items for our home and putting them to work. A few of my acquisitions include a little battery-powered vacuum for dusting our home office machines, a flashlight for practically every room, a simple intercom system for our most occupied rooms, a weather-alert radio, a videotape rewinder, a stapleless stapler, and a warmer for drinking mugs and small bowls of soup. Pretty practical stuff, I'd say.

I initially caught some flak, though, for the eight bucks I spent to install a second phone in our master bedroom. Oh, my wife and some of my friends gave me a great ribbing for that one. "Extravagant," "not practical," "silly," they said. "Funny!" they thought as they laughed.

But think about it for a minute: If you have one phone in a bedroom you share with someone else, and it's not cordless, who gets to answer any late-night phone calls? Who gets a phone cord across their neck if it's for the other bed occupant? Who always has to crawl over or walk around the bed to take or make a call if you're lounging with your mate?

Is the one nearest the phone always the best one to answer it—especially if a favorite show is on or one of you is dealing with a distressed kid? You may be chuckling at me, too; but I think I've got a case!

A while ago, a friend of mine got me to thinking about the role convenience plays in the everyday lives of people and how it might sometimes be more of a bane than a boon to our health and well-being.

Jim and I were attending a birthday party with our wives and a large group of the honoree's other friends at a local restaurant. Moments after I arrived, Jim asked if I could give him a ride a few blocks away to his own restaurant to retrieve a couple of essential personal items he had forgotten.

That was no problem. We hopped into my car and quickly made the 8-10-minute round trip. On the way back, though, Jim said, "I hope this doesn't make you lose your primo parking space." I said, "Hey, Jim, in the over-all scheme of things, that doesn't matter a whole lot. We can use it as an excuse to get a little exercise."

Jim said, "Yeah, you're right; but you'd be surprised at how important a convenient parking space is to the average restaurant customer!" We commiserated together a little more on how that could be a headache for restaurant owners, and then, just before we got back into the swing of the party, Jim said, "This sounds like a topic for an essay." So this one is for Jim AND because of his astute observations.

From time to time, I think we ought to examine our attitudes about convenience. We live in an "instant-on," "instant gratification," "remote control," "microwaveable," "portable," "mobile," "all the comforts of home… away from home" kind of society. Some of that's good; but some of it is slowly eroding our self-reliance, our creativity, our toughness, and even our health.

Depending on our ages, some of our parents, grandparents, or great-grandparents didn't have much to turn on instantly. They were gratified if they could get a letter from a friend or relative that was mailed two weeks before. They knew only the kind of remote control that occurred when people responded to a school, church or dinner bell heard across a neighborhood or a farm. The term "microwave" was not in their vocabularies. Restaurant convenience was miles away by a different sort of horse-powered conveyance than we have today; and a hitching post right in front of the eatery was not big on their list of requirements.

I believe we have the right to enjoy a more comfortable life today than did our foreparents, but we have to determine what our penchant for convenience may be costing us. Our attitudes may be influencing our children and the perception of members of a global society in adverse ways. After all, the rest of the world largely operates on a much different cultural norm than what American wealth affords many of us. Convenience and comfort are one thing (so to speak), but overindulgence and extravagance are another. A little inconvenience and discomfort now and again might remind us how privileged we are and compel us to promote a better life for the underprivileged.

WHAT I LEARNED WHEN I WAS ELEVEN
(BEYOND THE KINDERGARTEN BASICS)

I wonder sometimes if I was as smart as Robert Fulghum. You might recall that all he ever needed to know, he learned in kindergarten. Actually, I think we had the same kindergarten teacher...at least in spirit and principle. I also benefited early from that basic training about how to get along in a world populated by other people who are just as important as me.

In my way of thinking, however, my basic training was no more significant than my advanced training. For me, the advanced training came when I was about eleven. For some strange reason, the Universe chose for me a tender pre-pubescent condition as the appropriate time to instill some very important lessons.

One of these lessons was patience. Like most young children, I suppose I had trouble understanding why the world did not ask "How high?" whenever I commanded it to jump. It seemed that wanting something, and wanting it "now" should have been enough, and that complaining when satisfaction didn't come should definitely have been enough. When the bubble burst on that expectation, though, it did not come with a loud bang. Instead, my over-inflated child ego hissed out quietly like air through a pinhole in a balloon.

A church picnic was the occasion for my awakening. A number of our church members drove in a caravan to a picnic area that was located perhaps ten miles from our sanctuary along mostly gravel roads. For some reason, my mother and one or more of my three siblings and I made the trip as passengers in a car driven by our church's Minister of Music, Mrs. Brooks.

Of course, on a good day, ten miles might as well be a hundred for many kids. On this day, though, the distance was made to seem even longer by a dusty, zigzagged route down winding, country roads and a growing boy's growling stomach. Two o'clock in the afternoon was too far from breakfast. The trip seemed like a thousand miles.

Finally, I had had enough and from my location in the back seat, I blurted out, "I wish we'd hurry up and get there! I'm HUNGRY!" With a surprisingly calm voice, my mother replied, "Robert, just be patient. You'll get to eat."

For some reason, that quiet but firm admonition seeped into my consciousness like floodwaters slowly rising to engulf previously dry ground. One moment I was terribly impatient and concerned only with my seemingly unbearable hunger and the next moment found me realizing that all the impatience in the world was not going to get me to the picnic any faster than the drive would take…even if Mrs. Brooks hurried. The waters of realization were upon me before I fully knew what was happening.

It was a lesson I never forgot. I can't account for why it was learned in this way, but I know that my respect for the flow of life was never the same after that. I fully embraced the virtue of patience and somehow did it in a way that did not prevent me from learning assertiveness later on. But that's another story for another time.

If you'd like to know more about my advanced training, you'll just have to be…patient.

TOSSED SALAD: A VIEW OF A MULTICULTURAL AMERICA

The "melting pot" of American folklore becomes more or less synonymous with Gerber or Heinz Mixed Vegetables for babies if we begin with carrots, peas and corn instead of silver, gold and copper. Admittedly, that brownish mush has a taste and character all its own, but one would be hard put to guess which vegetables went into the blender before the final product came out.

I don't believe that America or the world will ever be culturally similar to pureed veggies. And frankly, I don't think we want that. But we certainly have to decide what we do want ... and who we want it for.

There are a few folks in this country who want America and the world to look like the produce department in the local supermarket. They advocate for cultural purity and racial segregation ... neat little antiseptic compartments for the potatoes, the eggplant, the onions, and the radishes. If they had their way, little white onions would grow up never even imagining little veggies as purple-black as an eggplant (and vice-versa.)

Then there are those who would advocate for vegetable stew. With a stew, all the vegetables lose some of their uniqueness and take on a little bit of the flavor and character of their stewmates.

But, have you ever noticed how vegetable stew is usually dominated by one of the vegetables? It's usually potatoes ... but that depends on who makes the stew. It could be carrots, or tomatoes, or green beans.

Stewies like that. As long as they're in control, or think they are, they tolerate other roots, fruits and tubers and eternally hope they can assimilate them.

But, wait! What about tossed salad? You can mix up anything in a tossed salad and douse it with American Salad Dressing instead of French or Blue Cheese. That way, every item can have a distinctly American flavor, but lettuce is still lettuce, and carrots are still carrots, and cherry peppers are still cherry peppers.

What a concept! A diner can bite into a TOMATO and let its tangy juice and firm red meat gush across the palate, or a cauliflower button and carrot slice can be chewed together and become "CAULICARROT" in the mouth. The salad means escape from vegetable monotony and an attempt at tasty cross-cultural mixing and matching of garden foods.

This is America... a multicultural America... an America replete with Latinos, Southeast Asians, "Orientals." Pacific Islanders, Europeans, Africans, African-Americans, Native Americans, and the list goes on. And within each of these broad-stroke cultural groups (and others) are greater diversities... innumerable ones. Such is the cultural produce department of the All-America supermarket.

We are all alike in that we are inherently, wonderfully human... different because of our unique human experiences, perspectives. and contributions. We are not all alike because we have the same basic skin color or because our forebears hailed from the same country or continent.

And yet, each of us wants to be safe and healthy, and loved, and happy, and productive, and successful, and fulfilled according to our own standards and definitions. None of us really want to see others without an opportunity for the same, nor do we really want to achieve those things for ourselves at the expense of others.

We are inching inescapably closer to a world of which many of us have dreamed—where we all can be judged by "the content of [our] character and not the color of [our] skins" (or any other superficial characteristic or stereotype).

As an African-American, I move through American society leading with the integrity of my character. I expect to be judged on that basis; and as a result, my experience tends to reflect my expectations. I am treated with the same dignity and respect that I afford others.

I know my own strength and power and I know that concerted effort towards my goals will bring me the successes for which I seek. I also realize, as Eleanor Roosevelt said, that *"no one can make [me] feel inferior without [my] consent."*

It has become my personal mission, then, to encourage everyone to affirm and realize their own stupendously powerful and fulfilling human potential; engender cultural cooperation rather than divisiveness; to celebrate diversity and not champion a homogenous culture; to teach that we push ourselves higher only by pushing everyone else higher; and to encourage all our unique contributions to the world.

When we exercise our freedom and discover our personal and cooperative power, we can achieve advancement for ourselves, our loved ones, and for the common good of all—without losing our identities.

"Lettuce" make America the "Tossed Salad Capital of the World." If we "turnip" our awareness, our collective human potential will "mushroom." We just need to "squash" the idea that we can't live in harmony together. We can definitely build a "24 carrot" society and enjoy the "grapes" of mirth. That's the way things were "mint" to have "bean," and you can't "beet" that.

I don't know about you, but my mouth waters just thinking about it!

AND NOW...FOR SOMETHING COMPLETELY DIFFERENT!

IMITATION OF LIFE

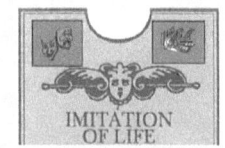

Preparing for the Real World
Via Creative Theatrics

Rob Simon

Life doesn't give us any do-overs...or does it? What if there were a way to practice some of the choices we make ahead of making them? Or what if we could watch someone else do it, and then critique their choices along with others who may have alternate ideas just as helpful as or even more useful than ours?

Enter creative theatrics, where the important idea is to merely reflect life in a way that gives the audience...and the performers ...a chance to learn important lessons that they might not otherwise have a safe opportunity to learn.

This is the purpose for **Imitation of Life**, where there are stories to tell, and models to mimic, and we ALL can produce them on stage, and learn from them together!

COMING SOON!
info@positiverhythm.org

If you enjoyed Inciting Reflection, there are three things you should know.

ONE...
This book was first born as radio commentary, and an Audible version of the book is in the works, with the plan being for the author to deliver the essays as he did originally!

TWO...
Author, **Rob Simon**, welcomes respectful dialogue about any of these ideas, or any of yours. For details, please visit the website below where you can engage with these musings directly.

THREE...
From the eleven-year period when Rob's essays aired, there are at least 400 that don't appear here...and the author hasn't put his thoughts on hold since. So...look at what's in the works! (And you can reserve a preview copy, and possibly be a select reviewer!
Model Cover Only

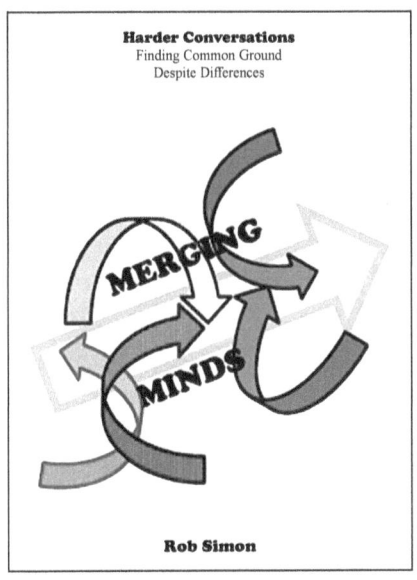

info@positiverhythm.org

www.ingramcontent.com/pod-product-compliance
Lightning Source LLC
Chambersburg PA
CBHW030115240426
43673CB00029B/485/J